IN
THE
WAKE
OF
DEATH

Surviving the Loss of a Child

IN

THE

WAKE

OF

DEATH

Surviving the Loss of a Child

Mark Cosman

MOYER BELL
Wakefield, Rhode Island & London

Published by Moyer Bell
Copyright © 1996 by Mark Cosman

Excerpts from the Los Angeles Times copyright 1991, Los Angeles Times. Reprinted by permission.

Excerpts from The Orange County Register reprinted with permission of The Orange County Register, copyrighted 1991.

First Edition

LIBRARY OF CONGRESS
CATALOGING IN PUBLICATION DATA

Cosman, Mark.
   In the wake of death: surviving the loss of a child / Mark Cosman. — 1st ed.
      p.   cm.
   1. Cosman, Berlyn, d. 1991. 2. Murder — California — La Crescenta — Case studies.
3. Teenage girls — California — La Crescenta — Case studies. I. Title
   HV6534.L26C67   1996
   364.1′523′0979493 — dc20   95-33400
                                                                        CIP

   ISBN 1-55921-157-1 Cl

Printed in the United States of America
Distributed in North America by Publishers Group West, P.O. Box 8843, Emeryville, CA 94662
800-788-3123 (in California 510-658-3453) and in Europe by Gazelle Book Services Ltd., Falcon
House, Queen Square, Lancaster LA1 1RN England 524-68765.

DEDICATED

TO

SUSAN

MORGAN

TERIAN

AND

BERLYN

1991

June 1, 1991

It is 9:30 Saturday evening when I turn into our driveway. The windows of our house are dark and uninviting. "Can't stay home for two minutes before she's off again," I grumble to my wife, Susan, in the passenger seat beside me. We had been looking forward to hearing all about our daughter's senior prom of the night before; I was even more eager to hear about the all-star basketball game she was to play in earlier today.

Morgan, our twelve-year-old daughter, awakens in the back seat when the car comes to a halt. Her pale blue basketball uniform is wrinkled and her big brown eyes are but narrow slits. She has slept all the way, exhausted from her own tournament in Santa Barbara. "Oh darn, Berlyn's not home yet," she sighs.

I climb the short steps to the double front doors, shove the key into the lock and notice a business card taped just below eye level. A note from Berlyn, I think. The living room is still and foreboding. I flip on the light and look down at the card. It is from the Anaheim

Police Department. There is a note on the reverse side. The handwriting is not Berlyn's. I set my bag of basketballs on the floor. Susan huddles close. Morgan flops down hard on the living room couch. "Who's it from Dad?" I strain to focus as I read.

"We are currently investigating a shooting in Anaheim involving your daughter (Berlin). She is at UCI Medical Center, Orange. Please call me for additional details. Thank you."

At first, I think Berlyn has been a witness to a shooting, perhaps a drive-by shooting outside her hotel. Not once do I think something awful has happened to her. I read the note out loud for Susan and Morgan. Sudden silence is followed by my wife's quivering voice. "Oh, my God. Mark, call the police. Call the policeman— What's-his-name."

I turn the card over, rush to the master bedroom, and dial the number. A tired-sounding, rough male voice tells me that the detective who left the card had long since left his office. I should contact UCI Medical Center. I quickly hang up and dial information for the number. It is then that I notice my fingers are trembling.

Is it Berlyn? I think for the first time. Was she wounded? I am beginning to enter a parent's most terrifying nightmare.

From behind me, I can hear a frantic exchange of whispers between Susan and Morgan. I dial once again and glance over my shoulder at Susan as I listen to a phone ring some fifty miles away. There is hope in her glistening eyes, but her expression has already begun to harden. Morgan holds the jersey of her uniform up to her mouth and stares hard at me. A voice comes on the line and I whip around to concentrate.

I quickly explain why I am calling.

"One moment, please."

A nurse in the emergency room comes on the line. Again, I explain who I am and why I am calling. There is an uncomfortable moment of silence before she directs my call further up the chain of authority. When the next person answers, I am again redirected. It worries me that no one is taking responsibility to tell me about Berlyn's condition. Why are they all passing the buck? Is the news that terrible? All I am able to learn is that she was admitted to the emergency room early this morning.

A woman's voice comes on the line announcing her title, some blend of social service and medicine, further arousing my fearful expectations. I ask her what has happened to Berlyn.

"The doctor who is treating her is not available, but I can have him call you in just a few . . ."

"Please," I beg. Heat spills into my cheeks as the sweat on my neck grows cold. "Tell me. Was she shot?"

A sigh comes from the receiver, followed by a conciliatory voice. "Yes, she was."

"Where? How bad is it?" I ask quickly, straining to listen over the wailing that suddenly erupts behind me.

"In the head. She is very, very critical."

We drive through the darkest night of our lives. Fear parches my throat. Morgan lies in the back seat crying, while Susan keeps begging God to make it all go away. I already know Berlyn is dead or, at best, that she is dying. I feel numb, as if I have been through it all before.

I suddenly realize that the path I am walking is going to divide, Berlyn going one way and I another. Strangely, it seems to me that the fork in the path has always been there waiting for us and that, somehow, I have always known it was up ahead. Now that it is only a few more moments away, coming to it seems almost anticlimactic. I am confused by my calm acceptance of what I knew was awaiting Berlyn and me at the hospital. We were going to part. I knew it was going to happen.

A tall young doctor meets us in the Intensive Care waiting room, along with the social service person I had spoken with on the phone. Unshaven stubble shadows his face, his bushy eyebrows pinch in a tired scowl. He wears a wrinkled green smock with matching trousers that bunch at his white tennis shoes.

We enter a small room midway down a brightly lit hall. Inside there is a desk with a phone, a couch and two soft chairs. Susan, Morgan and I huddle together on the couch. The doctor explains that Berlyn has been shot with a large caliber bullet; it entered through her left temple and exited through the back of her head. She had stopped breathing in the ambulance and, consequently, was connected to a machine that would breathe for her. Only her brain stem remained barely alive to keep her heart beating. The doctor suspected that it had been damaged by the tremendous shock wave generated by the projectile as it sped through her brain. It is only a matter of time before it, too, will surrender. Her brain is already dead.

"In cases like hers," the doctor continues, "there is no hope."

Somehow, his explanation does not move me. I had already accepted what had happened on the ride to the hospital. It is strange, but I am without emotion. I keep thinking it's as if my life has already taken another path, one that veers away from Berlyn's. I have already begun my solitary journey.

With the truth of her condition spelled out, the doctor leads us to a glass-partitioned room in the Intensive Care Unit further down the hall. Berlyn lies before us on a hospital bed with chrome rails drawn up around her. A plastic tube taped to her swollen face is connected to a bedside machine that hisses as it exhales into her lungs.

Her mother and sister hover over her, sobbing pleas for her to awaken. My only reaction is to withdraw—to be alone with the horror that fills the room. The crown of Berlyn's head has been hastily covered with a folded white towel to conceal the bullet hole.

My hands tremble against the bed rail. The machine keeps

hissing. For an instant, I try to sense what is engulfing me, but I cannot bring myself to face the impact. The moments bring back memories of when I was a child alone in the dark. Before falling asleep, I would often see shadows on the wall begin to shift and move as if they were attempting to form into something horrifying. I would lie there motionless, frozen with fear.

My eyes remain fixed upon my daughter. The hissing grows louder. Behind reddened lids, her beautiful blue eyes are shattered. Golden hair lies tangled and matted in a mix of blood and milky cerebral fluid. Only faint remnants of curls remain from the styling she was given before her prom. That was yesterday, in another life.

I reach down and hold her lifeless right hand. My brain is on overload. As bizarre as it seems, I remember a time when she was about four or five years old. We were at a special event. Ronald McDonald was there. Berlyn was standing on a parade float that elevated her to the clown's eye level. She placed her pudgy little hand on Ronald's shoulder and said, "It's okay, you can come to my house for supper. It's okay, you can come over." She looked at him seriously, as if he would have been devastated had she not invited him.

Now I rub her palm with my thumb. Just a month ago that hand held mine at her high school's father-daughter dance. Just four months ago that same hand received the year's Most Valuable Player trophy from the school's basketball coach, her third in a row. From that right hand came the results of the champion that was inside her.

She was a little more than average height for a girl of seventeen with a build that was strong but feminine. Her straight and true athletic frame, once so graceful and poised, lies stilled. She appears asleep, concealing her final ordeal.

Another memory flashes before my mind's eye. I see her walking to my car from across her high school campus earlier in the week. Her chin was always slightly raised, a sign of her dignity, I used to think. Now, in these last minutes, it is raised still, if ever so slightly.

It was only yesterday when she stood in front of the house in a shimmering green dress, her date by her side in a black tuxedo, patiently posing for my clumsy photo taking. I am rocked by the thought that her once happy spirit will never again dance upon the earth or race the wind across a field. I touch her face with the back of my hand. It is cold.

Now we trudge from the room. A concerned nurse drapes a blue blanket over Morgan's shoulders as we pass. She presses it against her eyes and cries. I steady Susan when I feel her knees buckle. She holds onto a metal railing and drags her shoulder along the wall as she sobs. The white-clad hospital staff can only stare at the remnants of this family.

I look back one last time as my heart says good bye. In the room behind us, the machine sighs, then stops, along with my daughter's heart.

Every metaphysical principle I ever learned rises up and swirls within my brain. Perhaps the sane life I once knew has continued on without me while my identity has become ensnared in a nightmare from which it cannot extricate itself.

June 3, 1991—Los Angeles Times by Marc Lacey
It was supposed to be the night of her life.
In anticipation of her senior prom Friday night, Berlyn Cosman, a pretty athletic 17-year-old at Crescenta Valley High School, had bought a green evening gown and gotten her long brown hair styled.
The all-star high school basketball player, her date and another friend took a limousine to the Hilton adjacent to Universal Studios and after dancing all night piled back in for a post-prom party at a hotel near Disneyland. There, she and a group of about 14 others rented three rooms, and there the fun—and Berlyn's life—came to a tragic end.

Berlyn was shot once in the head as she slept on a hotel room couch about 6 A.M. Saturday, allegedly by Paul—a former student at the school who dated one of Berlyn's teammates, authorities said. . . . Police say five other teens were in Room 608 of the Crown Royal Suites at the time of the shooting, but they are providing different stories.

[Berlyn] was a five-foot-eight guard who could deftly dribble past defenders, grab rebounds with ferocity, and shoot from beyond the three point line. She won numerous basketball honors, including The Times All-Glendale honors three years in a row, and played for a high school all-star team last summer that traveled to Hong Kong.

"She would go to school, race home, change into shorts and a sweat shirt and I wouldn't see her until dark," said her father, who frequently joined her in the pick-up games. "She would go to a park to play basketball every day. On weekends she'd be gone for five hours a day."

Daily News
"They all drove down to have a party in a hotel," (her father) said. "I was against it and so was her mom. But she said, " 'Daddy, this is the one time a year that I have to be on my own.'"

June 3, 1991

Susan, Morgan and I enter the lobby of the hotel where Berlyn was murdered. Once inside, we are dwarfed by a towering ten-story enclosed structure. The lobby is a sprawling indoor tropical garden complete with cascading waterfalls and exotic birds. The air is damp and warm. A stained-glass skylight looms high overhead. My eyes roam the tiers of suites, searching for the door to 608.

I walk to the registration desk. A young athletic-looking man in a maroon jacket smiles and welcomes me. "My daughter was murdered here two days ago," I tell him. His expression falls away and his eyes immediately leave mine to look down. "I've come to drive her car home and her mother and I want to see the room where she was killed."

He types something into a computer behind the counter and, without looking up, he asks if we will have a seat in the lobby. His rigid demeanor gives me the feeling I have triggered the hotel's legal alarm system. Susan sits on the couch across from me. There is anger in her expression like a veneer that is hardening over her sadness. I am not comfortable with the mood it creates in me.

An overweight middle-aged man with receding oily black hair and a worried look approaches from the indoor garden. He is wearing the hotel's standard gray slacks and maroon blazer. "Mr. Cosman?" he whispers as he pushes black rimmed glasses over the bridge of his nose. His expression is solemn, but the turmoil of the past couple of days is leaking through. He introduces himself as the hotel's manager.

He leads us inside an elevator with glass walls. We rise from the garden. Inside it is silent, but for the hum of the machine that is lifting us. No one is speaking. We step out onto the sixth floor where two young men in maroon blazers and gray slacks are waiting. We walk to room 608. The manager fumbles with a ring of keys. A bead of sweat trickles down from his temple. He grimaces.

We step inside the room after our escort. He stands off in the corner and clasps his hands behind him. The sofa-bed is unfolded, but there is no mattress. Standing by the door, I can picture Berlyn lying there vulnerable and exposed. My attention is taken by a massive blood stain on the mauve-colored carpet at the foot of the sofa-bed just in front of the large television cabinet.

I imagine paramedics loading her onto a gurney, the back of her head gushing blood and cerebral fluid. I can imagine the crowd of gawking students outside on the walkway peering in through the open door and bedside window. Sadness pours into my chest with the weight of liquid metal.

We take the route of her murderer on leaving the room, down the walkway, taking the elevator to the lobby and exiting into the parking lot. There, waiting for me, is Berlyn's little car, its grill seemingly a wide smile. It sits there like an obedient pet waiting patiently for its master.

In an instant I remember the day I gave the car to Berlyn. I had purchased it in Hollywood on a warm Saturday morning and parked it in the Burger King parking lot near our home that same afternoon. Susan had tied a big red bow on the steering wheel. Burger King was where Berlyn and I always went for ice tea after playing basketball at the park.

That evening after playing ball, Berlyn and I drove by our home to pick up Susan to go to Burger King. I could hardly suppress the grin that was pulling at my lips on seeing Berlyn's new car sitting there waiting for her.

We sat at a table by the big picture window overlooking the outside parking area. As if following a script, Berlyn began talking about how wonderful it would be if she had her own car. There was even a familiar whine to her tone.

"Okay," I said in a voice loud enough for nearby patrons to join in the unfolding drama, "I'm tired of listening to you harp to me about wanting a car." I pulled a key from my pocket and flipped it onto the table. "Here," I bellowed, "you can have any car this fits."

People around us suddenly stopped munching their burgers to study Berlyn's reactions. "Go ahead," I challenged her, "try it out. Whatever this key fits is yours." Her mouth fell open and her eyes widened. I could no longer hold back my grin. A broad smile lit up her face as her eyes turned slowly to the parking lot. She bolted outside to the applause of Burger King's customers. We all laughed together as she stuck the key into an array of car doors to no avail. She came back dejected. "It doesn't fit any of them, Dad." I could feel hot stares press against me from patrons and employees alike.

"Well, what kind of car have you been wanting?" I asked. She stood motionless for a moment, in deep thought, then her smile reappeared as her eyes drifted to the lone car sitting patiently in the very last row. "E-e-e-yikes!" she shrieked and raced back outside. I watched contentedly as she shoved the key into the lock and opened the door.

I look inside through the dusty back window. Berlyn's green prom dress lay over the back seat by her basketball. I put the key into the lock and open the door as she had that happy Saturday long ago. All that is missing is the joy, and Berlyn.

June 4, 1991—Los Angeles Times headline (by Marc Lacey):
School sets up a counseling center to help young people handle grief over the shooting of a girl and the arrest of an ex-football player.

Glendale News-Press
"Berlyn would pull the team together when certain players weren't pulling their own weight."
"She was the greatest. . . . She was my idol. My absolute idol."
"Prom night promised to be extra special for Berlyn because it was one of the only nights in her high school years that she was permitted to stay out past her midnight curfew. . . . The one night she stays out late, my God, look what happens."

Glendale News-Press
There is another town mourning the sudden death of Berlyn Cosman.
After graduating from Crescenta Valley High in June, Cosman wanted to spend the next four years of her life in St. Joseph, Mo. . . .
She was the only freshman-to-be recruited by Missouri Western State College coach Terry Ellis, who found out Sunday that Cosman had been shot to death. . . . "She was a lot more mature than a lot of kids we talked to her age. She knew she was going to be homesick, but

she thought it was something she wanted to do and that she could handle it."

Daily News
      Murder charges will be sought against a 19-year-old La Crescenta man in the shooting death of a high school senior who was asleep after an all-night prom party.

Glendale News-Press
      The halls of Crescenta Valley High School were astonishingly quiet Monday, as students reacted to the news that senior basketball star, Berlyn Cosman was dead.
      The school took on a quiet sense of eeriness that caused students who had not yet heard the news to realize that something was clearly wrong. "The school looked so different today," said freshman Heather Green. "It seemed like a place I'd never been."

June 5, 1991 - Glendale News-Press
      The annual Crescenta Valley High Seniors Awards program opened with a moment of silence for former classmate Berlyn Cosman. (Maria) Arias, said, . . . "she was a very bright girl and so smart. At least she loved life. At least she loved what she lived. For some (people) are always complaining about this or that, she loved her life."

June 6, 1991

Rags, Morgan's little dog, was hit by a car today on the street in front of our home. There were so many visitors and television crews coming and going along with the caterer setting up in the backyard that Rags had been overlooked in the confusion. As it turns out, he suffered a broken hip and lacerations, but he will live. I had given the dog to Morgan just last year during a party at actor Hugh O'Brian's home.

June 6, 1991—Daily News
A 19-year-old La Crescenta man said Wednesday that he didn't mean to shoot a Crescenta Valley High School senior. . . . "I just want to say it was an accident and say to everybody that knows me—trust me."
The teenager faces 20 years to life if he is found guilty of second-degree murder.

June 7, 1991—Glendale News-Press
To the Editor: The tragic death of La Crescenta co-ed Berlyn Cosman has saddened our community and deeply affected many of us whose lives were enriched and ennobled by our association and friendship with her.
One of those most deeply affected by the loss is my son, Nick Howe. He was a special friend who loved her deeply. Nick, a sophomore at USC, is in Canada working during the summer recess. On being told of Berlyn's death, his grief was inconsolable.

June 7, 1991

Today, I watch as they place Berlyn in a crypt. Behind her, they seal a marble panel. I will never again see her dance upon the earth. I am so sorry for us.

June 8, 1991—Daily News
More than 800 mourners filled a church to overflowing Friday. . . . After the funeral mass at Holy Redeemer Catholic Church, grief-stricken relatives and friends formed a 2-mile-long procession of cars to the entombment at Forest Lawn Memorial Park.

June 12, 1991

I return to work today, but it is more like a forced migration from the furies that descend upon me whenever I rest. I am vice president of the Volunteers of America of Los Angeles and president of its fund-raising arm, Friends of the Volunteers of America. Nationally, the organization has 6,000 employees in 37 states and some 200 communities nationwide, with many thousands more volunteers. This year alone, the organization will spend more than $300 million in bringing relief and a measure of dignity to those among us who find the way hard. My work has always been demanding. If anything can seize my attention from the storm that is raging around me, my job will.

I sit at the mahogany table that extends the length of our conference room on the fifteenth floor. Tall windows cover two exterior walls looking out over Los Angeles' Koreatown. I glance at my watch. A consultant is due in just a few minutes to give a presentation on the latest in management theory. My eyes drift over the nooks and crannies of the city as, behind them, memories of Berlyn's funeral rise from the dark recesses of my mind.

Close to a thousand mourners had attended. Men and women whose daughters I had coached, business acquaintances, high-school students—so many had come to say farewell. But a tall, lanky teenager, in particular, stood out from the crowd. He had been in the procession that passed before the casket, then by Susan, Morgan and me to offer condolences. The young man looked up at me from beneath his lowered brow and sheepishly extended his hand. He seemed ashamed, and defensively drew back when our eyes met. "Do you know who I am?" he asked in a halting voice. It was plain to see he was devastated. His eyes were reddened and glassy, his shirt wrinkled and his hair in disarray.

"Yes, I know," I responded to the brother of my daughter's murderer and slowly shook his hand. The procession seemed endless. Most of the proceedings were a blur, as if time had either accelerated or I had slowed. Only flashes of memory remain.

Following the funeral, many of our friends and family had returned home with us. The house and backyard were filled to capacity and then some. A nephew of mine from Texas, who was about twelve years old, tapped me on the elbow. He looked frightened and his words seemed stuck in his throat. "There's someone on the phone for you, Uncle," he said.

I squeezed through the crowd to the dining room phone. "Hello."

A rough, gravely voice responded. "Hail Satan, Mark Cosman. Hail Satan!"

The caller waited for my response. I could hear him breathing. I hung up. My mind riveted on the call I had received the night before. A different male voice, much lower in tone and with a slow, reviling cadence, had said, "I'm glad your daughter is dead." I remember feeling defiled, as if I had been drawn into someone else's nightmare.

My neighbor noticed the look of shock on my face.

"What happened? Who called you?" he asked.

I told him what happened. A few hours later, I received another call. My little nephew again came to fetch me from the backyard. He was trying not to cry. "There's another guy on the phone, Uncle. He's saying some scary stuff about the devil."

"I'll handle it," my neighbor said, his face red with anger, as he stormed into the house.

It was early evening by the time most of our guests left. Only close family members remained to help clean up. Suddenly, I began having terrible stomach cramps. It was as if all the tension I had locked within was gnawing through my insides to get out. Shooting pains increased in intensity until I was doubled over. Susan and her father took me to the hospital emergency room where the attending staff recognized me. They were very gentle and concerned. The doctor gave me a shot, but the demon within me fought it off. I thought of that terrible phone call.

I rocked from side to side on the gurney, whispering to Berlyn. I still had a lifetime to go without her. The doctor gave me another injection of something else. Slowly, the invisible hand loosened its grip on my stomach, but my sorrow remained.

Once home, Morgan came into the living room. She said there was a message on her answering machine that she wanted me to hear. I sensed more trouble. Will it ever stop? I asked myself. "Come on, Dad," she said in a disgusted tone, "You've gotta hear this."

My stomach still felt sore and I walked slightly stooped as I followed her into her room. She pressed the button on the machine and stood there looking at me as if I were at fault for what was about to happen. Susan joined us and moved in close to hear. After the long beep that separates calls, the disguised scratchy voice of one of Morgan's classmates squawked from the speaker. "This is Berlyn," the girl said, imitating a quivering, ghostly voice. "This is Berlyn. O-o-o-o, this is Berlyn."

I looked at Morgan. How cruel! Tears welled up in her eyes as she stood against the wall with her arms folded across her chest. Someone else had chipped away another piece of her heart.

Other staff members enter the room and take their places along the table. They are good people, every last one of them. I know it is hard for them to be themselves around me so soon after the murder. I sense they are simply waiting for me to heal, to be whoever I was before. But now I can never be. I am different now and I believe that difference will remain with me the rest of my life.

The consultant, an overweight man with a happy smile, walks briskly into the room, sporting a loosened red tie and a white shirt with rolled-up sleeves. I feel myself drift away on a dark cloud of sadness as he begins his presentation.

I involuntarily begin thinking about the young man who murdered our daughter. I do not have the rage or hatred for him I think I should. To me, he is a stooge, a pawn for the greater evil that used him to assassinate Berlyn. It is the evil, that great metaphysical force, that frightens me.

A sense of guilt builds, gnawing at me. My own reasoning is slowly connecting Berlyn's murder to causes that I have spawned. This connection produces unimaginable fear.

Is it something I did in life that set the gears of the universe in motion, resulting in Berlyn's horrible death? Perhaps I am being punished, I think, as the consultant's words melt together into monotonous background noise. I cannot explain my self-centered reasoning other than that it is simply out of my control. I want it to stop, but it will not.

Believing I am, in some remote way, responsible for Berlyn's death is subduing my rage against her accused murderer. How can I lash out at him when I am somehow his accomplice?

I think of how her murder has awakened unimaginable terror in me. Seeds of fear that had been planted in my childhood are now sprouting everywhere. All the while, my own reasoning nurtures the seedlings, giving them the sustenance needed to survive. At times, I feel like a spectator watching what is happening to the man I once knew to be me.

It is somewhere near the middle of the consultant's presentation when I suddenly return to the present and listen intently. He is talking about paradigms. A paradigm, he explains, is a model or pattern, but even more than that, it is a filter for our incoming experiences. Paradigms establish boundaries and create rules by which success is possible within those boundaries. The downside is that paradigms also require that all incoming data conform to its expectations.

A paradigm is like a god, I think to myself. By interpreting our perceptions, it controls everything. Perhaps it is my paradigm that is generating the guilt and terror I feel. Perhaps the origins of what I fear began ages ago when the human psyche was being formed.

I do not understand why, but I feel a passionate zeal to journey far into the history of our species, to the events that programmed the boundaries of the human paradigm. The idea that humans as well as computers can be programmed seems possible to me. Perhaps, in doing so, I will find and confront the origin of what frightens me. For now, I will occupy myself with the idea of the pilgrimage—soon enough I will be preoccupied with the trial of Berlyn's murderer.

The consultant provides a business example of a paradigm at work. It fascinates me. He explains that by 1968 watches made in Switzerland had garnered 65 percent of the world's market share and some 80 percent of the profits. At about that time, an obscure Swiss watchmaker invented a revolutionary new quartz movement electronic watch. He brought his remarkable invention before the rulers of the watchmaking industry, but the new timepiece had no mainspring or gears. It did not fit the established model of what a watch was supposed to be, and so the inventor's idea was rejected. With faith in his invention, the inventor continued to promote his unique new watch until it caught the eye of foreign electronic engineers. The rest of the story is well known. By 1978, Swiss watches had been reduced to only 10 percent of the world's market share and by 1981, most of the Swiss workers employed in the industry had lost their jobs.

June 29, 1991

I am perched on a steep rock ledge in the Angeles National Forest behind my home. A stiff breeze rushes against me. Behind, distant lightning bolts flash from dark seething clouds; ahead is a sun-drenched, unblemished sky.

I take a deep breath and am immediately enveloped by a delicate scent. It is unmistakably Berlyn's. I close my eyes and slowly breathe in her essence. The wind caresses my face as Berlyn seems to waft through me.

How wonderful to experience her again! Then, as quickly as she visits me, she vanishes. My eyes open to find a white butterfly bouncing along on the breeze in front of me.

The rest of the day I read from a book that was in Berlyn's purse the night she was murdered. It is *The Stranger* by Albert Camus, a story about an Englishman whose life had been relatively uneventful. Then, while walking along a beach in Morocco, he shoots and kills an Arab, for no apparent reason—or, at least, not one that would seem to match the crime. The principal character of the book describes how, when the gun went off in his hand, he knew his life had been changed forever. The existential essence of the tale comes from the macabre thoughts of the assailant during his incarceration following the senseless murder. I am amazed that Camus' story, of all others in the world, was the last Berlyn would read on earth.

I have read accounts whereby children, in particular, sense their own impending doom and, without realizing, reflect upon it in a variety of ways. Apparently, Berlyn was no exception.

Following the funeral, Berlyn's creative writing teacher had delivered a file to us that contained work Berlyn had done in her class. I have taken the file with me to the mountaintop. Among her papers, I find the following theme that she wrote only a month before her death.

Wednesday Writing

May 3, 1991

WHO AM I
By Berlyn Cosman

I am alone with no one. I am losing myself to the soil, the earth swallowing me in bits and pieces each day. My coldness is a normal thing, my hands open, wanting nothing more from the world I knew so little.

Who am I, you wonder. Why do you question me now? When I was in distress, no one came to save me. I fell so far, the seconds pass as hours and the darkness, the silence, the sudden disappearance of all that once was.

Now, I drift endlessly within invisible currents, bounding over the strange land like a tumbleweed. I no longer have roots, a place to be. I am no longer.

Who am I? I'm the infant you threw into the sea, the lost one no one wanted, the despised, the defeated. I am the one who found the way; the unacceptable, the poor among you, the dying, the one left behind.

On returning to the house, I sit in my backyard and gaze up at the stars, trying to fathom what has happened to my family. I have done this each night since the murder. A brilliant sunset, the last vestiges of volcanoes in Hawaii and the Philippines, yields to the night, giving way to a star-studded arch. There was a time when, on spectacular evenings like this these Berlyn would rush off to the beach just to sit and watch the sun set over the Pacific.

Since Berlyn's death, a strange planetary alignment has been unfolding with each night's sky. Jupiter, Mars and Venus have gravitated into a cluster just above the mountain to the northwest. Experts say that the remarkable phenomenon will not occur again for some two hundred years.

During the past few nights, Jupiter has broken from the cluster and is sailing away into the black void. Mars and Venus remain huddled close together. As I watch the celestial performance night after night, it appears as if the heavens are symbolically reenacting the dividing paths Berlyn and I experienced that terrible night at the hospital. Soon, Mars and Venus will separate and go about their solitary orbits. The performance will be over and the night sky will return to normal. Only the void will remain.

There had been other occurrences open to superstitious interpretation. For example, on my nightly walks through a neighboring park and baseball field, I would come across money. Mostly shiny new pennies, they were everywhere I walked. If I had chosen to, I could have filled the pockets of my jeans and still not taken them all. It was as if someone had taken handfuls of new pennies and thrown them like seeds where I walked. They were on the street, on the base paths of the ball field, along the paths I took—everywhere.

When I told Susan about my discoveries, bringing with me a few of the pennies to show her, she was not at all surprised. In her Southwestern Spanish traditions it is a sign that Berlyn visits the places where I walk.

I look up at the stars and remember what I was doing around six o'clock in the morning on the first day of June. I remember that I had gone to the apartment of a young girl to bring her with us to a basketball tournament in Santa Barbara. Susan accompanied me inside a stuccoed courtyard, while Morgan remained asleep in the car. A large black cat had shot out of a nearby bush and rubbed against my leg as it crossed my path. I remember sarcastically summoning Susan's attention, knowing her superstitious nature. "Hey look at this," I had said with a grin. She turned with a start and quickly made the sign of the cross. I remember chuckling to myself at her ingrained superstitions. Now it seems everything is open to doubt. I have little equilibrium beyond the security of my senses.

I remember the car I had purchased a month or so before Berlyn's murder. It was a black Mercedes coupe that came with a personalized license plate that read, Black Cat.

I am pondering these occurrences.

June 9, 1991 - Daily News
Partying and loud music brought police several times to the apartment complex where [the] high school dropout [who killed Berlyn Cosman] held parties on weekend nights while his widowed mother moonlighted to support her three sons, neighbors say.

The neighbors said they needed police help to quell loud parties at the two-bedroom townhome in a neighborhood of older, smaller houses tucked away in an affluent community.

June 19, 1991 - Glendale News-Press
Former Crescenta Valley High School football player Paul————— pleaded innocent Tuesday to the murder of Berlyn Cosman. . . . But Municipal Court Judge Roger Robbins refused to lower . . . $250,000 bail, despite pleas from his attorney that the 19-year-old defendant is not a danger to society and would not try to flee the area.

Friends . . . and his attorney have contended that the shooting, which was featured on the syndicated TV show "Hard Copy," was accidental.

June 29, 1991 - Daily News
A La Crescenta man will go on trial Aug. 12 in the fatal shooting of a 17-year-old girl.

Cosman and her date attended the May 31 prom at Universal

City, then rode in a limousine with several teenagers to a hotel in Anaheim.

July 2, 1991

It is Saturday. I go to the cemetery to be alone with Berlyn. We used to spend so many Saturdays together that, perhaps out of habit, I have to be with her for a while. Carrying a folding chair, I walk up the steps to her crypt atop the rolling hill. I run my fingers over the metal letters of her name on the plaque that is fastened to the marble panel. Her tangible remains are just inches behind the wall away from my touch. Below her name, the plaque reads:

BELOVED DAUGHTER AND SISTER
#33

So much has gone into the making of the famous number 33. I unfold the chair and sit down overlooking a spectacular view of the valley.

It seems like a dream, Berlyn. I remember when you were in the seventh grade and I had to get mad at you for not wanting to go to the park to learn to play basketball. I had hoped that, if you were able to be good at something—I mean really good—you would have been less susceptible to the kinds of people who prey upon kids with low self-esteem, you know, the drug peddlers and others who would lead you down the wrong path. I didn't have anything to offer you that would protect you when I wasn't around. But I did have a love for sports. So, I figured if I gave my love of sports to you, you would build something wonderful—for yourself—something that would give you pride.

Remember when I put together that little team from the girls in your seventh grade class and how I got us games against Catholic schools? We sure did get beat up pretty badly, but there was a dedication I saw in you that wasn't in the other girls. You were learning. You were like a bungling young lion cub learning what your instincts were for and how to use them.

Remember those cold early mornings at the park before school? The basketball would be wet with dew, cold and muddy. I recall one morning when your shots weren't hitting their mark. You must have been worried about something off the court or you just didn't feel well. You ceased to focus on your skills, indulging your anger instead. I became impatient and threw the ball down hard against the asphalt. "Look," I growled, "if you don't want to play just tell me."

You looked hard into my eyes and said, "Okay, I don't want to play."

"All right," I answered, "you've had your say, now get out there and play anyway!"

We looked at each other for a moment, then burst into laughter.

When you were having a problem with your game, how inspired you became when I would introduce you to a new move, a new shot or something that would add to your ability. Then, all of a sudden, you started to be *good*. Coaches from other teams were asking who you were. Not too long after, you became one of the best.

Did you know that one of the high school coaches you played against told me once that his team had a "Berlyn?"

"What was that?" I asked. He said it was a special defense designed just for you. He laughed when he told me that it never worked.

Hey, Berlyn, remember the night you scored thirty-five points and I went out and bought you that trophy with an inscription that read, *Man alive, thirty five!* Remember the game during your senior year when they put three girls on you? There were just a couple of seconds left and you hit that three-pointer to win the game, with those defenders hanging all over you. My heart leaped that night.

Then there was that game when your coach benched all the starters because of some infraction at practice that I can't even recall now. I remember how he finally put you girls in the second half. Wow, you were mad. But, you know something, that champion side of you wasn't going to be denied. When you went in the game, I could tell it was coming. I knew the look. You tore rebounds off the boards with a vengeance and then, oh, wow, then you hit all those three-pointers in a row. Even though we were playing out of town, you got the crowd behind you. They saw it, too. They saw that special quality in you that made you soar above the rest. The whole gym was rocking for you. What a night! The television news media played the video of those three-pointers on all the stations.

You know, I warned you about boys, about driving too fast, about drinking and that stuff, but I never thought to warn you about guns. I guess it was because when I was a teenager, guns weren't an issue. No one I knew had one. I'm sorry. It just never occurred to me to tell you that if some jerk shows up at a party with a gun, get out of there. Come home.

Well, your sister has a game today so I have to go coach. She's getting really good, you know. I just wanted to sit here for a while and talk to you again.

July 13, 1991

Morgan and Susan are in northern New Mexico in the embrace of Susan's family. I remain at home, having pressing issues at work. Two days ago, I was awakened from sleep by an eerie awareness that something was happening around me. It was about three o'clock in the morning and I was in that bizarre state between being awake and asleep. My eyes opened, but my brain seemed still in slumber.

Just then, I noticed one of Berlyn's old baby outfits, a short blue dress with matching suspenders, on the top edge of the door to my bedroom. I closed my eyes and opened them again. It was still there, standing upright as if being worn by an invisible child. Suddenly, the mirage leaped from the top edge of the door and traveled slowly across the room. It floated directly over my head and lit on the picture frame above my bed. In another moment, it glided back to its perch on the door and then vanished. I remember that dress because I had painted Morgan's portrait in it after she had inherited it from Berlyn. I remember how painstaking it was for me to recreate the outfit's folds.

Then my attention was drawn to the foot of my bed where a fountain of lights, composed of ascending bright round dots the size of golf balls, sprayed up and then curved downward before disappearing. The little round lights kept spewing from a source below my bed, each light following the one ahead of it until it extinguished. The pattern that formed reminded me of an infant sprout of new corn. I had no idea what the lights signified, if anything at all.

And yesterday morning, about three o'clock, I was again summoned from sleep. I immediately looked out the open bedroom door as if knowing exactly where to focus. Like the morning before, I was in that strange frontier between dreams and reality. The walls of the hallway and the room beyond suddenly disintegrated, giving way to a black, white and gray plane that was on a slightly different angle than the one on which I existed. It appeared to be tilted up from the far end.

There, on a crowded dance floor, I saw Berlyn smiling up at me, wrapped in the arms of a young man I had never before seen. She seemed in a state of absolute bliss. As if it were a natural occurrence, I simply laid my head back down on the pillow and reentered sleep.

This morning, at about the same time, I was awakened by the

same jolt of awareness. I looked out through the open doorway, as the hall and surrounding house silently fell away, yielding to that same black, white, and gray plane I had seen the morning before. Before my eyes lay a basketball court, surrounded by an arena. The stands were full of people. It seemed like a transmission from far away—the scene that emerged appeared grainy and the sounds were raspy like an old newsreel.

There she is, I thought to myself. Berlyn dribbled the ball down the right sideline in a silver uniform with dark gray numbers. There were young men on both teams. She pulled up her dribble by the baseline and with the grace only she possessed sent a high arching shot into the gray air. In another moment, the ball fell through the net to an explosion of cheers from the crowd. I watched in amazement as she raced up the court. Then, the vision dissolved, the house closed back together again and the visit was gone.

July 24, 1991

A circumstance surrounding Berlyn's death has just emerged and involves a friend of hers named Nick. He was a cinematography student at the University of Southern California and had dated Berlyn occasionally, but their separate paths to success had demanded so much of their time and dedication that they resigned themselves to a reunion farther down the road.

Nick had once told his mother that Berlyn was the girl he would marry one day. Nick's father is a successful movie director and he took as much pride in Nick's cinematic achievements as I did in Berlyn's ascent in basketball. To Berlyn, Nick had been someone with whom she found comfort and respect amidst the turbulence of growing up.

Nick had learned of Berlyn's death while he was working in

the mountains of Western Canada for the summer. He had become distraught over the murder and was distracted to the point of despondency. Just a few days following Berlyn's death, he had witnessed the aurora borealis, which he described as appearing to him as if heaven had opened.

Some days later, he was mountain climbing with a friend in rugged Canadian Rocky Mountain terrain when he became sidetracked, leaving the safer, recommended route. He happened upon a mountainside surface made slick by centuries of water run-off and apparently slipped on the smooth glazed rock and fell more than ninety feet to his death. The end for Nick came only forty-three days after the death of the girl he had vowed to marry.

Immediately upon hearing the news, Susan, Morgan and I went to Nick's home to offer comfort. Our families embraced, sharing an empathy for those who experience tragedy and then must live out the nightmares. Nick's camera had fallen with him. His mother showed us a pair of self-portraits Nick had taken on the mountain some time that day before he fell. Susan and I noticed the obvious sadness in his eyes. He was one of the good kids of this world. We will miss what Nick could have been to us.

July 30, 1991 - The Orange County Register
    Ninety minutes before he shot and killed Berlyn Cosman . . . Paul———— shouted obscenities at (her) and a female friend over whether he could party in their hotel room, newly released grand jury transcripts show. Voices: *"Don't mess with my baby. This is my gun, isn't it nice? It's a bad .357. . . . I don't care about you guys anymore. You guys are jerks. . . . I will steal a car if I have to. I've got my gun." Paul———— as quoted by Mitchell————.*

    "This is a guy that loves guns with a capital L. He loves them. This is a guy that needs the ego boost from having that gun. . . . (He) is missing something in his character and he bought it in the form of a

Smith and Wesson that night."

Chris Evans
Deputy District Attorney

July 30, 1991 - Burbank Leader
Glendale's Parks, Recreation and Community Services Commission will consider a recommendation . . . that a basketball court at Montrose Park used by Berlyn Cosman be named in her honor.

Although officials have named other local facilities after Babe Herman, Casey Stengel and other well-known residents, Nello Iacono (Glendale's Parks Director) said he believes this is the first time a basketball court has been dedicated to an individual.

"I think that would be the most wonderful tribute my daughter could have, to have youngsters and adults playing ball up there with her presence being known," said her father, Mark Cosman. "Many times when I'd get home from work, she'd be waiting for me and the first thing she'd say is 'Come on Dad, get your sneakers,' and we'd go play out there."

July 31, 1991 - The Foothill Leader
Several La Crescenta families were coping Monday with the second tragic death of a teenager the community has faced this summer.

Nicholas "Nick" T. Howe, 19, died Wednesday while hiking on Mount Rundel in Banff National Park, Alberta, Canada.

Howe . . . was a close friend of Berlyn Cosman. . . . "The only thing that makes us near being able to cope is the thought that the children are together," said Nick's mother, Beverly.

August 10, 1991 - The Foothill Leader
Orange County Superior Court Judge Theodore Millard denied a request to reduce the second-degree murder charge (of killing Berlyn Cosman) to manslaughter, which would have given him a maximum seven-year prison sentence if convicted.

Instead, Paul——could spend the rest of his life in jail if found guilty. . . .

August 13, 1991

Today, the city of Glendale dedicated a basketball court in Montrose Park to Berlyn. It was where she used to play each night after school during the off-season. The court lies atop a rolling grass-covered hill. How sad I had felt looking down at it from the funeral procession on the highway further up. Berlyn and I had spent so many exhilarating moments there. She was a pioneer; the first girl in town to play on a par with high school boys. When her shot was "on," she was remarkable. I remember the passes she made to me and the way we had counted on one another to do what we did best. I can still see her in the park, her silhouette bronzed by the setting sun, her ponytail bobbing behind her.

August 14, 1991 - Daily News
    A park basketball court where a pretty blond teenager used to practice jump shots with her father was dedicated Tuesday to the girl's memory with a bronze plaque. . . .

Glendale News Press
    A bronze plaque, 8 inches high and 12 inches long, with the inscription, "In memory of Berlyn Cosman, 1991," will be placed at the foot of the basketball pole, officials said.

Los Angeles Times by Catherine Gewertz
    The teenager who was sleeping next to high school basketball star Berlyn Cosman when she was fatally shot on prom night choked back tears Tuesday as he described seeing . . . the man accused of shooting her looming in the doorway just after the fatal shot was fired.
    Kenny Schaeffer, who took Cosman to the Crescenta Valley High School prom detailed the last moments of Cosman's life. . . . Schaeffer, 17, told the jury that he was sleeping . . . on a fold-out couch just before dawn on June 1 when the door opened, light streamed in and Javier Pimental, a friend of Paul's came into the room.

A moment later (the defendant) appeared in the doorway with a revolver, but Schaeffer said he "didn't think anything of it" because (Paul) had been waving the weapon all night. Schaeffer said he put his head back down on the mattress, but seconds later, he heard a gunshot.

Panic ripped through the room. As Pimental snapped on the light, Schaeffer bolted upright in bed, saying, "Where'd it go?"

"I looked down and I seen the blood coming from her, Schaeffer testified. [I said] 'She's been shot, she's been shot. . . .' I had a towel on Berlyn's head. I was yelling at her to breathe." Schaeffer said that as he picked up the phone to summon help he heard (Paul) say to his friend, Javier, "We gotta go, Jav."

September 16, 1991

Time moves relentlessly forward until I find myself sitting in a courtroom at the trial of Berlyn's assailant. I sit here amidst an entourage of television crews and tough-looking young adults who came in support of Berlyn's killer. I shake my head in disgust for even having to be here.

I am resigned to the fact that I have to represent Berlyn and piece together what happened to her during the last hours of her life. I had heard rumors, read many articles and had seen countless televised accounts about the tragedy, but media accounts were too impersonal, too removed. I want to listen to the testimonies and actually see the characters of this morose play so I can create an artificial memory of what had happened. The replay from my imagination will be all I have.

It was prom night. Berlyn, an honor student, had won a basketball scholarship to Missouri Western State College. The moment had come to release her grip on life, just a little, to leave the rigors of basketball and volumes of homework for a refreshing interval of fun. It was time to waste time, to test the budding independence she would need in college. At last, she had earned the right to make fun of it all, to laugh at what had been so serious for so long.

She attended a post-prom party in an Anaheim hotel near Disneyland with about fifteen other new graduates from her high school. Paul, a young man of nineteen who had dropped out of high school the year before, entered the festivities late in the evening with a few of his cronies. He was tall, strong and intimidating, his reputation as a dangerous troublemaker preceding him. The former football player and his friends brought weapons with them for a variety of bogus reasons. One of the reasons Paul gave was to protect a girl friend of his from her former boyfriend. Included in their arsenal was an assault shotgun with a pistol grip, a couple of pistols and Paul's special toy, a .357 magnum revolver. Throughout the night and early morning hours, Paul brandished the revolver.

At one point in the evening, he placed his gun on the table in the party room. A student asked if it was loaded. "No," he grumbled and immediately filled it with bullets. He flipped the chambers shut. "Now it is," he remarked in a provocative tone.

He waved the gun randomly at students milling about the room, then let his aim come to rest at a pretty co-ed who was standing with her date—a football player from the school's team. Paul mocked him saying, "Look at your girl friend, she's wasted." He walked toward the couple.

"Let me see it," the boyfriend said, referring to Paul's gun. "Don't—don't point it." The football player took the gun from Paul. Paul immediately pulled it back saying, "That's my baby. That's my bad .357."

Next, Paul turned his attention to a student who lay on his stomach on the floor watching television. He knelt down and rammed the muzzle of his revolver against the boy's buttocks. "Do you want your ass blown off?" he asked. "It's only loaded."

"No. Don't do that," the boy begged. "Don't mess around." Following the brief but embarrassing confrontation, the boy left the party.

Paul unloaded the weapon and dry fired it, taking random aim at students in the room. At one point, he even put the gun to his own temple and pulled the trigger. In spite of his claim of being inebriated beyond his ability to reason, at least at this point in the evening, he had the presence of mind to know when the gun was loaded and when it was not. After reloading the gun again, he cocked the hammer back, pointed it around the party room, saying how easy it would be to pull the trigger.

Paul's armed crony, Javier, approached the table. They spent a few minutes comparing weapons when one of the girls in the room became irritated with Paul. "Weapons and beer don't mix, you know," she barked. "Could you please put it away." Paul consented and unloaded his gun, placing the bullets in his pocket.

Later, about three in the morning, Paul and Javier proceeded to the party's quiet room, Suite 608, where Berlyn, her friend Jill and some boys were staying. Berlyn had an all-star basketball game later in the day, so she had to limit her celebrating and rest. Jill refused Javier and Paul permission to sleep in the quiet room. "You guys are going to go sleep in the car," she concluded. An argument ensued. Berlyn joined in support of Jill.

Paul's angry voice could be heard up the hall in the noisy party room, Suite 605. "Then, where am I going to sleep?" he shouted. "Fuck you, I want to stay here and party. I don't care if you're sleeping, let us just party in here." The door slammed. Paul stormed back into the party room. "I hate them," he growled angrily. "Fuck them, they're just dissing me. I hate them! I want to kill them." He slammed his fist against the table with his gun at his side. "Those fucking bitches. I hate those fucking bitches! I just want to kill them all!"

Berlyn and Jill's dates entered the party room to appease Paul, telling him he could stay in the quiet room if he wanted to, but Paul lashed back saying he no longer wanted to sleep there. He just wanted to go home. "I'll take Joey's truck if I have to, or I'll steal a car if I have to. I don't care any more. I don't care about you guys any more."

As the early morning hours wore on, Paul consumed more beer and continued his childish antics with his revolver. Then, for some reason known only to Paul, he stood up from where he was playing cards with his cronies at about six in the morning. He held his gun above his right shoulder and ceremoniously bid farewell to the tired celebrants. Then, with an armed companion he proceeded down the hall to the quiet room.

Paul's friend ventured into the darkened room first and made his way toward the washroom. Paul entered the room behind him. Light from the outside hallway splashed over Berlyn, who lay sleeping on a fold-out couch only a few feet from the door.

One sleepy student looked up and noticed the gun pointing out from Paul's hip. The student dropped his head back onto the pillow. Suddenly, an explosion ripped through the darkness. Berlyn never made a sound.

When police first arrived on the scene, the graduates reported that Berlyn had committed suicide. They had lied to cover for Paul who had long since fled the scene. The investigating detective had surmised that the group's misguided loyalties probably stemmed from their fear of Paul's intimidating gang-like entourage. When the police did not accept their account of how Berlyn was killed, the party-goers recanted, but they did so only as a ploy to continue to hide Paul. They brazenly went on with their subterfuge by presenting a new scenario about an unknown assailant who had barged into Berlyn's room and shot her.

It was not until the police brought their interrogation skills to bear that one of the new graduates finally came forth with the truth. Following his lead, the others stepped out from behind their smoke screens and named Paul as the one who had fired the gun.

It was apparent that the moment Paul ended Berlyn's life, she had no friends brave enough to speak for her. Not one. It was as if her life had meant nothing at all. In fact, one young woman at the party crowded into the quiet room just after the shooting. On seeing what had happened, she exclaimed, "Wow, what a bummer" and went back to bed. Later, the police had to reawaken her for questioning.

September 17, 1991

On the familiar long drive home from the Anaheim courthouse, I turn off the radio and open the sun roof. I want wind in my hair. I have to think, to try to fathom it all. The highway arches high above the ground. I look eastward. There it is. The fortress-like, pastel pink hotel where Berlyn was murdered. It sits alone, as if forlorn, on a stretch of undeveloped land near where highways converge.

I think of when Susan, Morgan and I stayed in a high-rise hotel across the street from the hospital the night Berlyn died. Susan was in the bathroom sobbing as she undressed to take a shower. She did not want to shower, but I had encouraged her to, hoping the warm water would soothe her. I happened upon her reflection in the bathroom mirror as I passed the half-opened door. I will never forget the look on her face; it pierced me. The once fun-loving girl I had met in college, the one who had found such joy in our relationship, had suddenly become someone else.

I used to think I could fulfill any need she had, even overcoming my foolish ways to earn her forgiveness for having hurt her. Now, there is a difference in the way she looks. Her elegant face is hardening with the sorrow that comes from being slapped by life. She can no longer absorb my errors or her own and still beam with delight. She cannot accept any more disappointments or confusing distortions of the life she had once expected. She has become furious with life and all who had used it to harm her. I realized then that our hearts had separated. Whatever cheap tales of romance pretend, grief does not unite.

I am quickly brought back to a time that seems not so long ago. I was a twenty-year-old student, walking up a hill to the administration building of a quaint little university nestled high in the Sangre De Cristo Mountains of northern New Mexico. Snow was piled shoulder high along the sidewalk. I turned a corner by the library and suddenly Susan entered my life. Long, coal-black hair hung down her back, her eyes were dark and exotic. Her chin was raised just a little, not disdainfully high, but high enough to give her a sense of purpose. Her black sweater and crimson skirt made her stand out all the more that day against the stark white backdrop.

She climbed the steps of the administration building, seemingly oblivious to my presence.

"Excuse me, Susan?"

She turned, whipping her shimmering hair over her shoulder.

"Are you Susan?" I asked.

"Yes." Her voice was dignified, her tone direct.

"My roommate said you do typing. He's a friend of yours— Rudy?"

"Yes," she said. "I know Rudy."

"Well," I said, as I pulled a manila envelope from inside my trench coat, "he said I'd find you here about this time. I need to have some typing done."

She walked back down the steps with her arms wrapped around a stack of books held to her chest, her Hispanic beauty becoming more apparent with each lithe step. I could see why the guys in the Kappa Fraternity had nominated her for Homecoming Queen. She was stunning.

She agreed to take the assignment for a hefty price, and completed it on time. However, when I turned the work into the professor, I found to my surprise that she had left out two pages. I received a failing grade, but I hoped that I could see her again. I looked her up at her dormitory and gave her another assignment, along with a request for a date. She agreed.

One date in particular stands out. It was early in the winter. We were attending a fraternity party in Gallinas Canyon, a rugged crevice in the forested mountains about ten miles from the university. A stone lodge at the base of a towering cliff was filled to overflowing with dancing, boisterous students. Inside, a roaring fire in an arched fireplace seemed to pulsate to the blaring music that emanated from speakers on either side. Three metal kegs of beer on a picnic table against the far wall were all but obscured by the crowd of students reaching in to fill Styrofoam cups.

Susan and I walked outside, bundled in heavy coats. She pressed her chin down against her white scarf. The bitter cold was heavy with the scent of mesquite that spewed from the chimney of the lodge. My breath turned to frosty vapor. Even the half moon looked frozen in the sky. We walked to a twenty-foot-high dam that spanned the narrow Gallinas River. Ice-crusted wisps of snow crackled and squeaked beneath our shoes. I took Susan's hand and held it inside my coat pocket.

We walked down into the dry river bed. Music dimmed in the distance, melting into the laughter behind us until only the beat was distinguishable. She leaned back against the rock dam and looked up at the brilliant array of stars. I was shivering as I took hold of the lapels of her jacket. She looked into my eyes without a word. I could all but feel her heart beat against my knuckles. I pressed against her and slowly brought my lips to hers. Suddenly, the night became soft and warm. Her sweet breath sighed against my face. I closed my eyes, savoring our first kiss.

Since the murder, Susan has often expressed bitter hatred for Paul. I don't share her feelings and I do not know why. At times, I even condemn myself for not having such focused hate. Yet I cannot shake the intuition that the murderer was duped, that he was a stooge swept into his own rage by a power greater than himself. He was not born to murder Berlyn. He had to have learned to do it along the way.

Recurring thoughts of the punishing vengeful God of the Old Testament spill into my tired mind. I dread them. They have taken on such a frightening reality since Berlyn's murder. Then, savage tales of ancient mythological gods that I had learned as a boy come to me. Through it all, concepts of evil that had been planted when I was young and vulnerable flash randomly through my head like lightning bolts in a storm.

As I drive on, I look to the west. The hospital where Berlyn died looms beside the highway. Across the street is the high-rise hotel where we spent that first night. Again I think of that first awful night. As I lay awake in those early morning hours, Morgan spoke briefly from her sleep—her words tore at my heart. "It's okay, Daddy," she said through a garbled sigh. "I'm going to sleep with Berlyn tonight. It's okay."

Whenever I find myself alone now, I become overwhelmed with metaphysical questions—where is Berlyn? who is she now?—questions for which I have no answers.

September 19, 1991

It is nearing the end of the trial. I enter the courtroom on the top floor of the high-rise courthouse and find that my usual front row seat has been taken by one of the many television cameramen covering the proceedings. I move to the front row across the aisle, which puts me directly behind Paul.

I sit awaiting the resumption of the trial when I hear the prosecutor's familiar voice behind me. "Just don't miss, Mark. I'll be up there too, ya know."

I turn around to find the deputy district attorney sitting beside a stern-looking bailiff. They are both staring hard at me. I am confused. "I don't understand. What do you . . . ?" Then it dawns on me. They think I have positioned myself behind Paul to assassinate him. "Do you actually think I moved over here to shoot Paul?"

"Yes," the prosecutor says flatly.

I lay my head back and laugh, thinking of the consultant's presentation about paradigms. I walked into the courtroom a businessman and, in the flash of a paradigm, I had become a stealthy assassin. It is the first time I have laughed since June first, and it feels good—however bizarre the inspiration.

September 24, 1991

Today the jury hears closing arguments. Near the end of the day, Chris, the prosecuting deputy district attorney, leans back from the prosecutor's table and whispers an invitation for me to visit with him in his office at the close of the proceedings. I have been in the courtroom each of the nine days at his request, a recognizable figure. He has wanted the jury to see that Berlyn was not just a victim, but that she was once a vibrant human being with a family who loved her.

Chris has done a masterful job. However, there is something about his previous suspicion of my intent to assassinate Paul that bothers me. He is a good and brilliant man, but his innocent naivete has been gnawed away by the contagion of the criminals against whom he has fought so valiantly. Their outlook—seeing life with suspicion, always on guard against a lie—has been transferred to him like a virus. I admire his courage and yet I feel sorry for the tremendous burden he has to carry in defending society from people like Paul.

Chris and I leave the courtroom together through a narrow corridor of jostling reporters and television camera crews. They clamor after us shouting questions until their voices are abruptly cut off by the closing elevator doors. In a few minutes, we step out into a windowless empty hallway below ground. It seems a sinister place, where the destruction of so many desperate lives has been plotted, where evil has collided with human society. The thick brick walls seem to ooze sorrow.

We weave through the maze of hallways and turn into his office. "Oops," he exclaims with an embarrassed scowl. "I should have done a little house cleaning before I invited you down here."

I notice the life-size mannikin against the far wall of his tiny cubicle office. A red dowel runs through its head, depicting the path the bullet had taken through Berlyn's skull. Paul's black revolver lays on Chris's desk, along with the other weapons confiscated at the party. A blood-stained bedspread is rolled up in an open brown paper bag on the floor. "Are you all right with this?" he asks concerned.

"Yes, I'm okay." I have an insatiable appetite to see and touch anything related to the last seconds of Berlyn's life. "Do you have the bullet?"

"Are you sure?"

I nod. He opens his drawer and hands me a palm-sized metal container. I open the lid and there it is, the mangled projectile that killed my daughter. I hold it in my hand for a minute or two, then hand it back. "May I see the photos?"

"Oh, Mark, you don't want to see those. Let me tell you, she did not look good in death."

"Please." I ask again as I pick up Paul's revolver and run my hands over its dull black surface. I feel the rough spots where rust has gathered from exposure to moisture. Paul had hastily hidden the gun beneath some shrubs on the hotel grounds as he fled the murder scene.

Chris reluctantly reaches into a cardboard box on the floor by his chair and hands me a couple of eight-by-ten-inch photos of Berlyn that had been taken after the murder. I will never forget them.

Seeing them for the first and only time reminds me of the day they were introduced as exhibits during the trial. They had to be shown to Paul as a matter of course. I remember seeing him glance at the photos from the corner of his eye and quickly turn away as if the sight horrified him.

Chris leans back in his swivel desk chair that squeaks and clasps his hands behind his head. "Well, how do you think we did?"

We discuss the case, but my mind is still reeling from what I have just seen. I want to close my eyes and be alone, but I have to perform. That is what makes the days after Berlyn's death so tiring—I have to function no matter how I feel inside.

It is late when I return home. I find Susan sitting in the living room with her arm draped around Morgan. They have been crying. Her mother died of cancer earlier this day.

September 26, 1991

The jury has reached a verdict. Paul is found guilty of second-degree murder. He will be sentenced November first.

When I arrive home, I hear the phone ringing just as I put the key in the lock. I rush inside to answer it.

"Hello, Mr. Cosman?" It is a young woman's voice.

"Yes." Another reporter, I think, or perhaps one of Berlyn's friends.

"Were you at the trial today?" she asks politely.

"Yes, I was. Who . . . ?"

"Well, I hope you're happy now, you son of a bitch," she says and hangs up.

September 27, 1991 - Los Angeles Times by Mark Pinsky

After deliberating just one day, a jury on Thursday convicted Paul———of second-degree murder. . . . "It was the only decision we could make," jury foreman Paul H. Swan, 49, of Anaheim said outside court. "None of us liked it."

Prosecutors had argued that a drunken defendant shot Cosman because she had ordered him out of her room so she could sleep. Paul's attorney, E. Bonnie Marshall, argued that Cosman's death was a tragic accident, that an intoxicated [defendant] had stumbled into the darkened room while trying to place his pistol into his waistband, discharging the weapon. Marshall said an appeal was likely.

When the verdict was read, Paul showed no emotion, but various members of his family wept quietly.

Glendale News Press

Orange County Superior Court Judge Theodore Millard called the case a "true tragedy" and said [the] 19-year-old defendant . . . was "a time bomb ready to go off, unfortunately he went off that morning."

[Paul] . . . dressed in an orange jail jump suit and tennis shoes, didn't show any emotion during the sentencing.

October 1, 1991

My plane lands in St. Petersburg, Russia, and taxies to a small square building at the far reaches of the runway. I sit awaiting instructions from a husky female flight attendant standing by the bulkhead door. Six soldiers, armed with automatic weapons, circle the jet. Baggage handlers in dirty blue shirts and red caps begin unloading luggage.

My thoughts turn to an event that happened months ago.

I had promoted a major fund-raising dinner honoring famed entrepreneur R.E. (Ted) Turner in recognition of his pioneering efforts in Soviet-American relations. At the gala, Charlton Heston, together with Sergie Ivanko of the then-Soviet Embassy, the late Dr. Armand Hammer and Michael King of King World presented Mr. Turner with the first-ever Glasnost Award. Proceeds from the tribute were earmarked for use by the Volunteers of America to provide entrepreneurial training for Russian youth, shifting the hopes and aspirations of these youngsters from a controlled economy to one that was struggling to become market based.

The occasion had been one of the last public appearances by Jill Ireland with her husband, Charles Bronson. With her arm resting on her husband's, she labored up a flight of stairs to the predinner reception. *Paparazzi* lined the way, their flashes dazzled my eyes. Jill had paused halfway up the short flight of stairs, and with the dignity of royalty, she raised her chin, turned to the throng of photographers and smiled, hiding her need to rest behind a pose. Charles stood proudly at her side with his usual strong silent demeanor. Jill died of cancer just a few weeks later.

The event also marked the first public appearance of Jane Fonda with Ted Turner. The renowned author Dominick Dunne was also there. I did not realize it at the time, but his daughter had also been brutally murdered.

My thoughts return to Berlyn. I feel myself sink deeper into the seat. I have a week of meetings and television interviews ahead of me that I have to endure. I need to concentrate. At night, there will be welcome moments in my hotel when I will be alone with my thoughts. They will be my oases.

Now we are led from the plane through an outdoor hallway of tall concrete walls that block any a view of the airport complex— lingering vestiges of Soviet paranoia. The early evening sky is gray, the air moist and cold. Inside the reception building, the window panes are painted black. I wonder why they had bothered to install windows in the first place.

Following an inspection of my passport and visa, I am taken, along with other passengers, to a dilapidated school bus that hauls us away to the main terminal. There, I am met by Artak, a doctor on the staff of the Kirov Institute in St. Petersburg. Artak will help me establish a committee of influential Russians to begin education for budding entrepreneurs in St. Petersburg.

Artak is in his early forties, of average height and build, with dark hair combed over a balding crown. His tan trench coat opens to a gray suit and white shirt. He walks briskly toward me, side-stepping luggage, and extends his hand. He does not know about Berlyn.

A limousine takes us to downtown St. Petersburg. "I want to show you the problems we are facing," he says in a heavy Russian accent as the driver pulls over to the curb. I step outside. There is something unsettling about the night air. It is the same feeling that disturbed me the night I came home and found the detective's note on my door. I push the intuition away until later. I have to function.

Artak leads the way down a dark crowded sidewalk to what appears to be an ill-kept bakery. Its windows are streaked with grease and covered with steam. From its tall doors, a long line of people in suits and work overalls—executives and tradesmen alike— snake into the darkness of a side street.

"They wait for hours," Artak says in a sympathetic tone.

"There is no bread. Come, I will show you." We pass through the pressing stares of people in line and enter the store. Row upon row of wooden racks are empty. Only three loaves of unwrapped bread are left.

"We will cross the street to the other market," Artak says nodding his head toward the door.

We wait for an antiquated trolley to rumble past. Blue-green sparks spit down from overhead wires. Silent somber workers stand crowded together inside. The scene has a surreal quality. I wonder if it is just the different reality in which I find myself, or has life, itself, become alien since Berlyn's murder. I am in a daze. I only hope it is not evident to Artak.

"You see," Artak continues, "it is the same here. There is no meat." We walk down a long line of somber people and enter a state-owned butcher shop. Inside the dimly lit eighteenth-century building, a row of refrigerated display cases are empty but for a small tray of a half-dozen fish, each only about eight inches long. Wooden shelves on the wall behind the display cases are empty except for the three large dusty jars containing something fermented. The air is rancid.

That evening, I lie in bed looking out at the Neva River from my window on the ninth floor. Just up the thoroughfare is the Czar's Winter Palace, where Nicholas and Alexandra, along with their children, were kidnapped by revolutionaries, who later murdered them.

Tall cranes that no longer lift anything poke up from the city's floor. They seem like theatrical props; there is virtually no construction in the city. There are no high rises or other modern architectural triumphs aspiring upwards. It is all flat and gray.

Later in the week, after finishing a television interview, I am having dinner in a restaurant with Artak and a colleague of his named Boris, a psychologist who was once assigned to the Soviet space program. He speaks limited English, so Artak helps him along.

Boris is tall and lean with receding gray hair, a long pock-marked face and a perpetual grin, as if he were suppressing a chuckle from a joke heard earlier. He seems to welcome my questions and when the subject leaves business for more philosophical realms, his eyes brighten. It is during one of these departures from the mundane that he relates a puzzling story.

Boris had been the personal psychologist for several cosmonauts. One, in particular, had ventured farther into space than any of his comrades. The fellow, one of the originators of the Soviet space program related to Boris that he had experienced a phenomenon that had forever changed his life. During his mission alone in space, he claimed to have been visited by the spirits of his ancestors who, he had said, wafted through his space capsule. Boris went on to say that the cosmonaut knew each one, not by name, but by feeling. He recognized them as being connected to him genetically, though they had come from many earlier generations. The shocking experience brought him, according to Artak's translation, "to the end of himself."

I await elaboration, but Artak has finished. He bends over his soup plate to sip from his spoon. I sit dumbfounded for a moment. Boris looks up at me and smiles. There is wisdom in his silence. The wily old veteran of mental wars is welcoming my need. He senses it; I know he does.

"What can a person do when he is at the end of himself?" I ask.

He begins speaking in Russian. Artak starts to translate, but Boris raises his hand to stop him while looking hard into my eyes. He wants to say the words himself to convey their intended impact. He sits still for a moment grinning to himself and then he leans out at me and says, "It will pass. It will always pass."

October 12, 1991

Back home, warm Santa Ana winds rush down from the mountains, carrying the parched scent of the high desert. My thoughts turn involuntarily to Berlyn's murder and how it has shattered everything in which I had once believed. The greatest destruction is to my concept of God, which for so long was at the center of my life. It is now in shambles.

If God is omniscient, as I had been taught, then he had to have known Berlyn was going to be murdered. If he is omnipresent, he had to have been in the quiet room with Berlyn and Paul. If he is omnipotent, he had the power to stop the murder. And if he is all loving, he certainly would have. Evidently, the concepts of God I have carried through life have been naively misleading. I am suddenly left without spiritual equilibrium.

There is another terrible consequence of Berlyn's death. It is an unbridled fear that has dominated my reasoning. I fear evil, which I had been taught was in opposition to God. But God, evil and fear all seem interconnected to me now. All the logic my mind can muster is focusing upon Berlyn's murder. There has to be a reason that it was Berlyn who was murdered at the party and not someone else. My concepts of God and evil are entangled in the event and it frightens me.

Worse still, I feel I am beyond the help of all other humans. The powers I face alone are at the foundations of the universe itself. However irrational it seems—even to me—I am terrified that, by my own fault, I have unlocked a metaphysical gear in the universe that has ultimately brought about Berlyn's death. And the gear is turning still.

I am in desperate need to embark upon an inner pilgrimage to the origins of God and evil and the fear they spawn. If I am to understand what they really are, rather than what I have been led to believe they are, I must. In so doing, I hope to flee my shattered paradigm for a new universe in which I can search for what has become of Berlyn if, indeed, she has become anything at all.

Like all kids, Berlyn lived her life from the sandbox to the classroom trying to earn the acceptance of her peers. From an early age, she had learned to share with other children, to give them what they wanted so she could co-exist. She learned to dress for their approval, to mimic their jargon and all the rest of the things youngsters do to be acceptable to the society in which they find themselves. Then one of them slaughtered her on a whim.

A kind of human I had never experienced before has barged into my view of life. I begin to feel an aversion for society altogether. I wish only to be an observer, a bystander among people. I no longer want to be a member of the tribe that has killed an innocent, loving creature. I want to separate myself from all other humans.

Following Berlyn's death, many well-meaning people came to offer their counsel. Some had suggested that perhaps Berlyn's murder was in punishment for an occurrence in a previous lifetime.

Such a view seems terribly unfair to me. How can a person be punished for an act about which he now knows nothing? I thought. It makes one's current life hopelessly fatalistic. What kind of God would devise punishments for mischief performed in a different body, under different circumstances, for different reasons and by a different human identity?

Others attributed Berlyn's murder to an act of God that must be fearfully and faithfully accepted without question. My Western heritage is steeped in fear and trembling where God is concerned. This outlook has always bothered me. The same God that would turn a human being into a pillar of salt or discard a transgressor into a lake of fire was also purported to be humanity's loving father. Secretly, I never really understood how the two diverse personality traits complemented one another.

I presume many of us have thought about the nature of evil in our time, either as a real and viable force in the universe, or as a cloak for the acts of humans. Deep in the foundations of my paradigm is the scary notion that a dark power directed Paul to Berlyn's room and used him to kill her.

What always concerns me about the reality of evil, at least in Judeo/Christian terms, is that if everything that exists is issued from God, and if God is perfectly good, then from what source did evil spawn?

A fundamentalist Christian visited me in my study earlier this evening. She said that Berlyn was now in the arms of Jesus. I asked where Jesus was when Paul aimed his gun at Berlyn's head and pulled the trigger. "We have free will," she responded with self-assurance, "God never interferes with our free will. It is His gift to us that He would have to take back if He took control of our lives."

I wondered how the same kind of thinking always allowed God's positive interference—better known as miracles—in man's free will.

This woman's theology was safe and comforting as long as it went untested by reality. I was beginning to sense that her answers to my dilemma were fulfilling a need she possessed. She was being the instrument her authority figures said she had to be in order to win God's favor. Every question of life had a biblically referenced answer. When answers did not fit the gravity of the question, unflinching faith became her order.

To argue a point with her would have made me feel uncomfortable. To me she was doing what she had to do for her own well-being. I have been in that position before, straining to fulfill a role rather than being myself. Oddly enough, I began to shed my own depression, to relate to her need for a solid mechanical universe designed and operated by a loving God, who knew us all by name. I suspect it is a hope many of us have had at some point in our lives.

On the other end of the spectrum, I had the opportunity to speak with a highly regarded neurosurgeon who had lost his only son in an auto accident a year before Berlyn's death. When I asked him if he had found any metaphysical reasons why his son had been killed, he explained that to question such events is fruitless. He described man as analogous to a single-cell bacteria living in the intestine of God. How could the bacteria understand the creature who is its host, let alone occurrences outside the universe of the host's body?

The doctor's answer gave me the feeling of being helplessly insignificant. I also felt a pang of self-incrimination for my brazen lack of humility. Who was I to demand answers from life?

Yet, it seems to me that to explore life, to evolve and improve, is at the very nature of all living things. To simply drift means, for me, an end to becoming.

I will have to rummage through the twisted rubble of my theology later. Right now, the most burdensome task that confronts me is continually to fend off my fear of somehow having been the metaphysical cause of Berlyn's death. When I hear or read something that, on the surface, seems unrelated, my mind often contorts the meaning to feed the guilt my soul harbors. Such setbacks leave me floundering for days in depression.

On second thought, perhaps I will not have to suspend rummaging through the ruins of my theology. It is becoming increasingly obvious to me that my concept of the struggle between God and evil are at the foundation of my fear in the first place.

October 13, 1991

As I am packing away some of Berlyn's keep sakes, a childhood snapshot of me slips out from one of her scrapbooks onto the garage floor. I pick it up. In the photograph, I am about the age of two, reaching out to pat a patient cocker spaniel that sits in lush green grass. I have a wide grin on my face.

The photo gives me pause. I look inward, watching the walls of my assumptions slowly rising around me. I had just enough roaming space to think I was free. Scholars and fools had ventured inside the walls to counsel me, but I sensed they had come for their own reasons, rather than for me, as they had pretended. Then came the "surgeons"—religion's proprietors—who implanted fear's reactive ignitions. They even took away my vision by turning my eyes in upon myself. I no longer saw life for what it was, but only what I judged it to be.

I pick up Berlyn's high-school world history textbook and slowly flip through the pages she had read, stopping occasionally to read what she had underscored. As I browse through human history, it becomes increasingly obvious to me that the influence of learned assumptions has been so great as to have caused the ebb and flow of even the mightiest civilizations.

I turn to the Aztec empire and think of how the great Aztec king Montezuma relinquished his empire to Hernán Cortés. Long before Cortés, there had been a white-bearded god who had visited the land we now call Mexico. Like Cortés, he had come from the east by sea and, in time, became the great Quetzalcoatl of Aztec legend, also known as the Plumed Serpent.

Though most all written records of Quetzalcoatl's rule were lost to history, his legend still remains. Zealous Catholic friars, following Spanish soldiers like scavenger fish behind a school of sharks, had destroyed all records and depictions they could find of the ancient ruler—answering the call of their own paradigm.

According to legend, however, Quetzalcoatl ruled the precursors of the Aztec people. A golden age emerged from his reign until, for reasons unknown, he left his people and sailed eastward from where he had come, vowing to return. A heavenly sign was to herald his coming.

Near the time when Cortés stepped from a boat onto the Aztec empire, a comet had streaked across the night sky. On seeing the celestial event and coupling it to other facets of Quetzalcoatl's legend, Montezuma assumed that the end of life as he knew it had come.

As a result, Montezuma welcomed Cortés into Tenochtitlán, the Aztec capital, to take his rightful place within the Aztec paradigm. I believe the great king had no other choice. To me, he had to obey the paradigm that had perpetuated it all. The rest is history. Montezuma was betrayed by Cortés, held hostage and later stoned to death by his own people.

And my paradigm? All the observations I ever made about life have been done from its parapets. What I really observed, I will never know. Everything is interpreted as something else. Nothing is ever neutral; it is all judged. It has been the way in to me for everything I ever knew and, now that it is in ruin, it will be my way out.

With reverence, I place Berlyn's book in a box and bring one of her scrapbooks onto my lap. Around me, the garage has become a quiet peaceful cocoon in which I can be alone with the remnants of my daughter's life. I open the book to a picture of the two of us. We are standing together, my arm around her shoulders, her head resting against my chest. The photograph was taken only last Christmas. The expression on her face is one of peaceful content-ment. "What happened to us?" I ask her as she stands there looking out at me from the photograph.

I find that whenever a cataclysmic disaster strikes, the players involved must personalize the tragedy by discovering what made it happen. More importantly, I had to know why the tragedy hap-pened to him or her in particular—why me rather than another? In effect, even tragedy, however horrible, must be woven into the surviving victim's beliefs and understandings. In the mind's desperate search for causes to weave into effects, even once belittled superstitions rise up and take their place beside scientific fact, vying for a place in the living tapestry.

I turn the pages of the scrapbook to a wedding picture of Susan and me. It is then that I think of how my past was strewn with potential causes that, metaphysically, implicate me in Berlyn's murder. Scarlet threads of guilt are becoming increasingly predominant in my living tapestry.

Like so many young people, I lived my youth in a torrent of becoming. I did not know the severity of my mistakes until their effects eventually bore into my heart.

To begin, Berlyn's mother and I met at a university where we became caught up in a whirlwind romance. Like so many impetuous youthful relationships, our responsibilities to one another were to have fun and maintain good enough grades to stay in school so we could have more fun.

But reality arrived in the birth of a child—our child. For different reasons mixed with confusion, we decided to offer the child for adoption—a decision we would come to regret the rest of our lives.

I looked into Susan's eyes that day when we discovered she was pregnant and saw the sadness and trouble I felt I had put there. She had been a gift I had abused and now was throwing away. My selfishness had risen and stared back at me through my mind's eye. It was an awful thing to behold. I blocked it out by thinking that if I could just put this one experience behind me, the future would be what I wanted. And I would be wrong about that, too.

Tugging at me was the love I felt blossoming in me for Susan—I couldn't bear the thought of her having to suffer the embarrassment and hardships alone. So, I promised to stand by her through the ordeal.

Thinking there could be an end to something left undone was my greatest misconception. The effects of our decision would never end. Mysterious consequences would always be out there stalking us. For me, I had discovered the road that bearers of foolish decisions are doomed to take. Sometimes, when I look back, I feel a snap of pain in my heart.

To carry out my promise, I retreated with Susan to Massachusetts near my childhood home and the sacred woods where the terrain was familiar.

There it was—the cause my psyche needed to intertwine Berlyn's murder with me. It fit into the pattern I had been weaving with precision since my youth. Berlyn had been taken in retribution for my having given away my firstborn. I had rediscovered an old fear of a vengeful God who stood at the gates of my world.

There was no escaping what I had done. The difference is, years ago, I did not know what I did was wrong. Now it is starkly evident. What have I reaped from my folly? The answer had suddenly come alive, bursting from the barrel of a pistol.

I had not thought of that child given up for adoption as being the cause of anything in my life before, but with the storm that followed Berlyn's murder, she had become an effect. For me that child confirmed my assumptions about how life worked: My mind needed a reason for Berlyn's murder and, morally, the daughter I had betrayed fit the terrifying puzzle with precision. Whether correct in my assumptions or not, like Montezuma, I was bound to fulfill my role in whatever belief I had in how life operated. For Susan, there was no doubt—God's long-awaited punishment had finally come.

I thought of Susan's image in the bathroom mirror at the hotel the night Berlyn died. In reality, she has had to endure the loss of two daughters. Her look that night had reflected that unfathomable pain.

Susan enters the garage carrying a hamper full of laundry. I look up. "Hi."

"Hi. What are you doing?" she asks mechanically, without glancing my way.

"Just going through some of Berlyn's mementos. Would you like to see some?"

Her expression hardens. "Not right now." She sets down the load and reenters the house. There was a time, not too long ago, when she would have beamed her beautiful smile at me and sat by my side even if it meant pretending to be interested in what I was doing. Will the passage of time help us? It seems certain that I cannot.

After surfacing from a long bout with the depression of grief, the last thing either of us can bear is the other's lamentations. As a result, we struggle as best we can in our separate ways. If there was something either of us could do for the other, we would, but it seems that allowing the other person to be alone with grief is at present the best antidote.

I suddenly recall our migration from the university to Massachusetts, where I could take care of her. We had no money to begin with, so during her pregnancy, I worked two jobs and she worked full-time for a temporary agency. In the daytime, I was a guard in an inner-city jail and at night, I stood at a lathe, carving rifle barrels from blue steel at Colt Firearms Company. I drove from one job to another, often falling asleep at traffic lights.

The jail building has long since been demolished; the three-story redstone complex was nearly one hundred years old. There was a room next to the infirmary in which there were three metal cells, the size of shower stalls. Inside the stalls, metal cuffs and leg irons were bolted to the walls. It was where they once shackled violent inmates.

At the jail, I was put in charge of a ten-bed infirmary that was under the direction of a rotund little doctor who held sick call twice a week for two hours. He usually wore suspenders under a brightly patterned sport coat and always had a long cigar stuck in his mouth. It was a dreadful place. I work to erase the thoughts from my mind.

October 15, 1991

I bring one of Berlyn's scrapbooks to bed with me. As I turn the pages, I come to a picture of Morgan in a scary Halloween costume. Only a few weeks before Berlyn's murder I had come home from the office early to find that a life-sized effigy, the likeness of a scarecrow, had been placed at our front door. The sadistic grin on its papier-mache face hinted that its creator knew something I did not. At the time, I had supposed it had been placed there as a mischievous prank. But when I had looked down at Berlyn's broken body in the hospital I saw a fleeting glimpse of the scarecrow-like figure in my mind's eye.

Compounding my metaphysical speculation, on the same day that I had found the effigy I also found a dead pigeon on our front lawn. The incident does not sound like much, but the bird was not lying on its back or side, as one might expect. Nor was it mutilated in any way. I found it sitting there facing the effigy, its wings tucked in against its sides.

So great was the impact of Berlyn's murder that unbridled panic rushed in from everywhere. In response, reason used anything it could find to dam the tear in the universe through which chaos poured. The effigy was just one of the things reason quickly grasped and stuffed into the hole.

Perhaps, reason surmised, the hideous creation had been a

warning or a curse placed there by a twisted human steeped in the occult. I never believed in such possibilities, but the magnitude of the tragedy destroyed what I held to be truth. As a result, new life was given to the possibility of what I had once believed to be lies. Such is the way tragedy casts its effect far beyond the truth of what it is.

The mystery of the effigy and the fear it wrought homed into receptive targets that had been planted in my paradigm long ago. In the vulnerable days of my youth, the surgeons warned me of invisible demons that shared our universe and operated from within evil men. The bridge across the abyss to Berlyn's murder was not only transporting events from the past, but also superstitions— reason's demons had crawled up from the darkness and were crossing over as well.

If my case is prototypical, whether a man believes a set of teachings or not is without consequence when the self he has made is overwhelmed. I have learned that when the self is in a state of utter confusion and cannot respond to life, even old questions, fears and doubts, long believed conquered, resurface and become significant. It seems that even former childhood concerns reappear to haunt once again. Such is the path to insanity, the ultimate loss of identity.

Life, for me, is becoming a trap from which there is no reprieve. All the while, living moments are moving relentlessly forward, away from Berlyn.

I close my eyes. It is not long before I relax and am somewhat removed from the world around me. But it doesn't last. As I feared, the moment I am at rest the thought that I had somehow caused Berlyn's murder rushes at me from the darkest reaches of my mind. I am becoming exhausted from the repetitive attacks. The macabre fear is always near, lurking in the shadows.

This time I stop right where I am to make a stand and begin to reason against my reasoning. If Berlyn had been a victim of what I had done in years past—giving away a child, for example—then other parents with similar histories would also have suffered the murder of a subsequent child. But that clearly was not the case.

It would also be possible that murders the world over were actually punishments wrought by a manifested metaphysical law or vengeful God. Following my reasoning further, murder would then become a holy act.

I am beginning to understand what I did not realize I had learned many years ago when I was in the tutelage of society and religion. The foundations of my life have surged up from my subconscious with the wild cataclysm of events and I am shocked by what I find. According to my former way of thinking, every passenger killed in a catastrophic airplane crash, for example, could be linked to a transgression of socio/religious principle. A blind force would have had to select victims with equally weighted transgressions, brought them together and killed them without regard to mitigating circumstances or present state of mind.

I think of the floods that have killed hundreds, famines that have brought agonizing death to thousands and wars that have slaughtered millions. As groups, the victims of these tragedies become only impersonal numbers. To the families of these numbers, the horror of the event is deeply personal. For them, randomness becomes a pattern and the universe a frightening black hole into which the light of their lives is lost.

I also consider victims of tragedy from the vast array of cultures and religions that differ from my Western traditions. From the most primitive of men to the most advanced, the vision for living life permits behavior in one religion or culture that would be condemned by another. If morality is linked to metaphysical cause, I wonder to what universal moral standard humanity is being held accountable.

I once thought there was one all-encompassing changeless archetype against which all choices were compared, in order to judge right from wrong, good from evil. It must have been the same didactic thinking missionaries employed when they supplanted other religions with their own.

Reality now appears different. It seems more relative than I had once thought, to the point of being neutral but for the characteristics assigned it by judgments of the beholder. It is evident that Western man's archetype is starkly different from, for example, a Zulu warrior's. One could suffer the brunt of guilt for an action that, to another, might be perfectly acceptable.

So many questions I long harbored but evidently ignored are surfacing with the foundations of my life.

It is becoming apparent to me that however insignificant my religious and social heritage may have seemed, the terrible fear with which the teachings were planted remain like dormant seeds. A catastrophic event that may last but a second is all that is required for these seeds to sprout their furies, bearing even more power than when I knew them as a child. The accompanying guilt seems directly proportional to the magnitude of the tragedy to which it is associated. I could not have created greater burdens to carry than those provided by my own reason.

October 16, 1991

I am awakened by the sound of weeping. Susan rolls over in bed, turning her back to me. I reach over and gently rub the nape of her neck. "I know." There is nothing more I can say. I have said it all on other sleepless nights. Words do not mean much to us anymore. I look up at the pattern of gray shadows on the plaster ceiling. I guess it's because we once used words that never really worked to explain philosophy and religion, or maybe it's because words convinced her to put our firstborn up for adoption. Who knows? The only certainty between us is that words have lost their impact.

I recall the day I left Susan at the hospital to return to one of my jobs. Our daughter was born that day, but as it worked out, I would not see her face. The nurses on Susan's floor stared disapprovingly at me as I walked down the hall from her room. I knew they hated me for the decision I had made. Their feelings were obvious. I was tired from working so many hours and depressed from the ordeal; their disdain hardly mattered. In time I would condemn myself far more effectively than they could anyway.

After only a few more months we found ourselves embracing at the airport and saying good-bye. That dark day I watched her plane ascend into the clouds until it disappeared. The chapter was over. I felt hollow inside. I could only imagine how Susan felt all alone on that plane.

As time passed, my moments apart from Susan seemed in vain. I had found that she had given added value to my dreams and aspirations rather than detracting from them. Without her, I was missing an important interpreter, a different perspective through which to view life. What good would success be if it is not shared? I asked myself. What measure is there for experience? Susan had become that measure for me. Whatever she enjoyed, I most often did too, not because of the experience necessarily, but because it brought joy to the one I loved. If I were able to give her happiness, it made me feel good in return. Only my search for God and the meaning of my life remained private.

We stayed in touch by phone during the long time apart. Her parents never knew she had been pregnant or had given our child away. It was the way such things were often done in those days. Now, having had the time to convene with myself and discover what I wanted, without demands pressing in on me from every side,

I found that I wanted to share life with Susan. I felt elated on the one hand for recognizing the need and saddened on the other for not having found out in time for our lost child.

Respecting her father's Old World traditions, I wrote to him and asked his permission to marry Susan. He gave us his blessing. He was a hard-working man with a kind heart. I liked him. If there are saints from the practical world, he would surely be one. Joyfully, Susan returned to New England, where we were married.

We lived in Hingham, Massachusetts, near the sea. Our first year was like a continuous honeymoon. We were inseparable. I would do nothing in which Susan did not have a part. I went to a little grocery store in the village one day during a snow storm. The owner, a balding Italian man with a bloodied white apron and a broad smile asked, "Hey, where's your sidekick?" That was the way it was for us. We rarely went anywhere separately, except to work.

The August night came when we decided to leave the magic of our honeymoon and return to the university to finish our educations. We made the decision while sitting together on a boulder high above an ink-black sea. Susan and I were having those strange dreams experienced by some college students where we found ourselves walking past a classroom with neat rows of students inside diligently at work. In the dream, it would then suddenly dawn on us that it was a class we were supposed to have been attending since the beginning of the semester—but had somehow forgotten. Finals were usually the next day and we were hopelessly behind.

We could hear surf and smell salt in the air. A lonesome foghorn sounded from deep within the distant dark night. A single gull answered the call. It started to drizzle, but it did not matter. We were together and in love. What is more, now we were about to embark upon an exciting adventure together.

We worked until we had saved enough money for our tuitions.

Then Susan and I piled everything we owned into the back seat of a compact car and headed for New Mexico.

Susan rolls onto her back. A tear channels down from the corner of her eye. "Oh, I saw Berlyn so clearly," she sobs. "I dreamed her as a little child again. She was sitting on the couch and when she looked up and smiled at me, my heart broke. Oh, why did he have to shoot her? I loved her so much." I am stung, for I am powerless to help her. There is nothing I can do other than listen. I put my arm under her head. "Why has my life turned out this way?" she asks. "This isn't what I wanted. I never had trouble like this when I was growing up."

My heart sinks. The way she says it suggests to my fragile ego that I might be the cause of the tragedies that have befallen her. Her life had been without sorrow until I happened on the scene and then a whole cataclysm of terrible events seemed to begin. Perhaps metaphysically or karmically there is something terribly wrong with me. I feel like the devil himself. The connection between Susan's sorrow and the answer my guilt demands might not be logical, but in the absence of time-tested answers I can trust, it is all I have.

On nights like these, I find myself escaping to times when Susan and I believed in each other and were very much in love. I am sure we still are, but our attention turns inward rather than to one another.

On one summer day, several years after we had graduated from the university, I left a telethon I was producing in El Paso, Texas, and rushed to the hospital where Berlyn was being born. Back at the show, the masters of ceremonies were asking for pledges per pound of Berlyn's birth weight from parents in the viewing audience.

I walked the hallway to Susan's room. Nurses smiled at me as I passed. What a change from six years before I remember thinking.

Many of the televisions in the rooms I passed were tuned to the telethon. Turning the corner, I stopped in my tracks. Susan was being pushed toward me on a stretcher from the recovery room. Her doctor, a kind elderly man in operating room scrubs, was walking alongside. He saw me and grinned. The short Hispanic orderly behind the gurney maneuvered to a slow stop. Susan was crying. I looked up at the doctor, thinking something had gone wrong. "She's just happy. That's all. She's just really happy," he chuckled, and patted her on the wrist.

I kissed Susan on the forehead and held her hand. "Berlyn is down that hall on the right. You'll be able to see her through the window," the doctor said. Susan did not say a word. She was simply overcome with happiness. I kissed her again and told her I loved her. The orderly wheeled her away.

I found my way to the newborn nursery. There were two rows of infants wrapped in blankets, in baskets, with only the tops of their tiny heads facing the visitor's window. As I was scanning the rows, I saw what appeared to be a yellow light flash from the head of the second infant from the left in the second row. It turned out to be Berlyn.

October 17, 1991

Thoughts of Paul invade my mind. I envision him in his cell, of how it will be for him there and it reminds me again of my jail days.

Our inmate population was about three hundred men. On sick-call day the line in the hall outside the infirmary averaged about one hundred fifty jittery inmates seeking medication. Drugs were currency for them, the stuff of favors. The doctor knew it, but it was better to medicate them than to face their hostilities.

October 19, 1991

I am in the garage sealing away the last of Berlyn's things at the bottom of a box. I come upon an old black-and-white photograph of my childhood home I had given her. It apparently had slipped from one of her scrapbooks.

I am preoccupied with the need to find the origins of my concepts of God and evil and the terrible fear they prompt. I want to start there, at the beginning, and challenge everything I have learned along the way until I reach the new universe and Berlyn.

The rational self I have woven could never accomplish the journey, but there is someone within me who I think can. I used to find this entity in the woods behind my childhood home when I was a little boy.

I sit on a stack of boxes, resting my back against the wall, and recall a time long ago. There I was, probably about six years old lying in the snow atop a frozen pond. Clumps of ice clung to my frayed mittens. Ear flaps hung down from my cap, hugging my ears. Above me was an opening in the forest's canopy through which I focused upon a bright pinpoint in the heavens—evening's first star. A fiery red sunset had cooled to deep purple. Behind me, the forest was darkening. There was magic in the air.

Joy raced up my spine and stung the tip of my nose, my eyes welled up with emotion. Something within me was happy to be alive. It was more like an alien mentor than a little boy's personality. It felt life with my hands, observed it through my eyes and listened to its sweet familiar sounds through my ears, but it was far greater than I. It seemed to have transcended the ages to be with me and, as a result, I was special. I called it The Watcher.

Sometimes when I was alone, I felt the alien watching me from outside myself. I did not know if other kids shared the same experience. I was too afraid of their judgment to ask. I did not speak to The Watcher nor did I ever see it, but I would often feel its presence.

I rolled over onto my stomach and brushed the snow from the pond's crystal surface. There, suspended in the ice just below my nose was a large goldfish waiting for the spring thaw.

The Watcher had been my friend long before the last seemingly insurmountable wall had been erected around me by the humans. In those magical days when I was young, it would peer over the parapets of my world calling for me to come out and play in the field with no fences. I will ask The Watcher to take the journey with me to the new universe.

I do not remember exactly where my concept of God came from. My family was not religious. I suspect, however, the concept came to me as I compared my own experience with what I had been taught by the proprietors of religion and that ranged from hearsay to Sunday school. My concepts must have started early in life, during the time when we lived in a three-room tar-papered house on the outskirts of a New England forest.

As I lie on the soft snow-covered floor of the sacred forest, my eyes study the darkening sky. A soft, halting voice floats into my silent pine-scented realm.

"Honey, are you in th-th-th-there? It's about t-t-t-t-time fo-fo-fo-fo-for Da-Da-Da-Da-Daddy to ca-ca-ca-ca-come home." My mother is peering in from the edge of the forest. Fog rises up from the snow and bathes her in the pink haze. She is a pretty woman with hazel eyes, fair skin and shoulder-length dark hair.

I come to my feet, my green wool jacket matted with snow. There is always an expression of sadness on Mother's face and a telltale sigh that ends her broken words. She smiles in at me, then seems to gaze into the dark reaches of infinity. I have seen that stare many times before.

*   *   *

On a frigid winter night four years earlier, I had become very ill, my temperature skyrocketed. A strong child, I managed to fight off the disease. The virus migrated in search of a weaker host and found one—my brother. The next day, Jay was overcome by fever. My father had denied Mom's appeal to take him to the hospital. With his small construction business in its infancy, my dad was without resources for emergencies. And, besides, Jay was not his child, but a son inherited from Mom's teenage marriage.

So, with Mom at his bedside through that fateful night, Jay battled gallantly against the disease that had first attacked me. By morning, it became evident that he was losing the struggle.

A worried-looking doctor came to our shanty early that morning. Angered by Jay's condition he immediately took him to a hospital in the city. Mom had prayed for Jay's deliverance, but it never came. In a few days the fever ended, but in its place a deafening silence arrived. Jay never came home again that year. Instead, he was exiled far from his mother—the only friend he had in the world—to a school for the deaf.

Jay's misfortune would stalk him through his childhood as if it were a living creature bent on his destruction. Because the disease that defeated him was first mine, it seemed that a pattern for his misery was set in motion. I would always be intertwined with my brother in a guilt-ridden relationship that found me surviving at his expense.

Life was not something my mother conquered, I thought, but something with which she compromised. It seemed even the gods were mocking her—she could not speak and now her firstborn could not hear.

Whether genetically or otherwise, I inherited my mother's affliction, and I entered school a stutterer. Needless to say, school was a grueling ordeal.

I could not accept my condition. To me, it was a curse, like Jay's deafness. I hid from it when I could, willing to exchange failing grades in school for dignity. When there was no way out of a situation, I stood and fought, facing my nemesis head on, but I never won. Whatever it was, stuttering had more control over certain situations than I seemed to have.

I remember sitting at my desk in a fifth-grade classroom. The tall graying woman at the front of the room was randomly selecting students to read and diagram sentences she had written on the blackboard. I cautiously drew my clenched hands through a puddle of sweat that had formed beneath them on my desk. I stiffened and became motionless like a hunted animal exposed in barren terrain. Harsh sunlight streaked through the towering windows. Slowly, I unfastened the decorative gold-plated stickpin from my tie and slipped it into my desk, lest it reflect a ray of sunlight that might catch the teacher's attention.

I did not know what God was in those early days, but I had heard stories so, in desperation, I prayed to be delivered from stuttering. I hid behind the student in front of me, whispering prayers of deliverance, frantically trying to put the right words together that would save me. I guess it was there, in the classroom, that my interaction with God, however desperate, first began. People from different walks of life, strangers and friends, had taught me that God was in control, so I naively asked him to rescue me from my dilemma. They also said he was vengeful—a superhuman father who punished his children. They told me he threw the worst of his children into a lake of fire somewhere deep within the earth where they would burn forever. Fear began to creep into my thinking.

When my prayers went unanswered and I was continually trapped in situations where I stuttered, I naturally concluded I was at fault—I was one of God's bad children. I believe it was then that

I first began the war inside myself against what I learned was sin. For me, the origins of guilt began in the classroom, along with my concept of God. It seems now that one continually fed upon the other—one needed the other to survive.

Then I was told God was also loving and merciful and would forgive my boyhood transgressions. If only I repented, he would spare me from his terrifying lake of fire. So, steeped in sin, I groveled for forgiveness as I crouched behind my desk afraid to move.

Seared in my brain is the memory of the teacher's disdainful look, as if she were looking at the infectious wounds of a leper. Her thick, painted lips pronounced the directive. "You there," she said sternly, pointing a pale, bony finger at me as baggy white skin swayed beneath her arm.

I sat up straight. The students pivoted in their seats, sporting gawking wide-eyed grins, awaiting the bizarre struggle they knew was about to happen. "Do number seven," she demanded.

In those days, the hardest words for me to say began with the letter "s." My clothing felt like sandpaper against my skin, my throat tightened like a vise. I riveted on the sentence, appalled by the mockery it represented of my mute plea. It read, "The silent submarine slipped slowly away." I struggled and contorted, but I could not speak. Not even with the teacher's impatient demands for me to get hold of myself could I force myself through even the first syllable.

I walked the five miles home that day with my head bowed low, thinking about what had happened to me and assessing how seriously I had been damaged by it all.

Over time, I became rebellious. When there was an oral exercise in class that came without warning, I would do something wildly comical, enough to have me thrown out of class. I spent many days as a problem student in the principal's office, but I had saved what was most important to me at the time—my dignity. If I was going to be made a mockery of, then I would dictate the circumstances and the manner by which it would be done.

I was elected class clown and recorded as such in our class annual. It must have seemed fitting to my classmates, but they never knew the agony behind their laughter.

I do not stutter anymore, having overcome most situations at the base of the stuttering pyramid out of, perhaps, a sheer need to survive. There are still situations at the very tip of the pyramid that are difficult for me, but they are rare.

October 21, 1991

I finish an appointment at a hotel near the beach in Santa Monica, and take some time out for me, to walk on the hard sand at the surf's edge. The air is heavy, wet and sweet with brine, the sky gray. As I walk along, I think about a late summer day following my tenth birthday.

Dad was driving me home from a sand lot baseball game at the village field. By now, Dad's business had grown dramatically. He took a long puff from his cigar and exhaled a ring of smoke that swirled against the steering wheel. "You played a hell of a game, kid."

I looked up into his stern face and grinned. I was proud of my dad. He was lean and handsome and a great coach. Whatever problems he and Mom were having seemed to be in their adult world—something I did not understand. I sensed that the way I played baseball made him happy. I loved the thrill that came with excelling before a crowd.

We turned into the long dirt drive toward our little house tucked against the woods. We passed the wooden skeleton of our new home, a work in progress, on the grassy knoll. I remember bending forward to look out Dad's window at the field of amber grass to the west of the forest. Enchanting thoughts returned of the deep, cold brook that lay just beyond, and my many adventures there.

The car stopped. I climbed out with my dilapidated baseball glove in hand and suddenly froze. A husky, overweight boy of fourteen stepped clumsily from the porch. "It's Jay," I hollered. "Jay's home!"

A hearing aid plug that received only faint vibrations mushroomed conspicuously from Jay's left ear. A flesh-colored wire ran down from the apparatus to a bulge in the pocket of his gray shirt. His sandy hair was cut short.

Warm, laughing eyes naively betrayed his happiness to be home. I approached cautiously. Jay giggled aloud, dispelling my fears that we had become distant relatives during his long exiles. In a childish attempt to overcome our confusing relationship, I grabbed his hand and shook it exuberantly. Just then, Dad passed, glancing warily from the corner of his eye. After an awkward self-conscious wave, he focused his gaze on the ground and walked into the house. For a fleeting instant, his image as a coach and stern patriarch had yielded to a man embroiled in guilt. Jay waved back, but his smile had vanished. He knew he was unwanted.

Jay awakened early the next morning, eager for any plans I might have for the day. He ate breakfast with Mom, savoring precious moments spun from dreams. Thoughts of having to return to school in three weeks had been tucked away with the strange anonymity he must have felt.

I remember lying in bed listening to Jay's slurred guttural voice. "Dean Lanzger smacked my wrist with a ruler for not being on time to her class. I swore at her, Mom. They sent me to my room for three days on bread and water. They didn't give me supper until everyone else had eaten."

"Pla-Pla-Pla-Pla-Please t-t-t-try to b-b-b-behave. Can't you have sa-sa-sa-sa-someone ca-ca-ca-ca-call me when you're in tra-tra-tra-tra-trouble?"

"No, they won't let me. Oh, please don't send me back there. Please, Mom, I think I can read lips well enough to go to public school now."

I sprang out of bed at the sound of Mom's voice cracking. I walked into the room, fastening my bathrobe. Jay bolted excitedly from his chair, his cocoa-stained T-shirt half-tucked into baggy khaki pants. "Hi! What do ya wanna do today?" he asked excitedly.

Mom left the table to hide her tears and stood staring out the kitchen window. A faint high-pitched moan eked out on a sigh. I wondered why our little family had to suffer so much.

"Some kids are coming over to practice baseball—want to play?" It was all I had to say. Jay ran into our bedroom to change. Mom looked back at me with reddened eyes and forced a smile. I remember asking myself again: Why was Jay so impaired? Why was Mom tortured so? To me, in those early days of childhood, God was life itself. There was no separation between them. I had yet to cover life with a concept and give it a human personality.

Jay's life in an institution had not taught him how to participate in normal boyhood fun; recreation had always been a structured affair with proper adult supervision. As a result, his reliance on my leadership simply widened the gap between us. Jay was older and, under normal circumstances, should have led me into the adventure of boyhood. But, now like a good-natured clumsy oaf, he followed after me in everything we did together.

Dew still clung to the grass as I hurled batting practice balls to my friends in the field next to the little house. A tough-looking boy of fourteen smacked a sharp grounder toward Jay at second base. Jay grimaced with determination and groaned aloud as he went for the ball. Suddenly, the bounding sphere hit a rut, jumped up and smashed him in the mouth. Blood spattered from his lower lip, but he would not be deterred. There was too much at stake. Grunting with irritation at his own awkwardness, he turned to throw and stumbled over backwards; damage done to his inner ears had also robbed him of balance.

The tragic look on his face as he lay face up in defeat spoke for itself. Finally, he stood up and brushed the dirt from his trousers, still mumbling words of self-chastisement.

By this time, the neighborhood gang was caught in a fit of laughter, pointing fingers of mockery at me. What happened to Jay rubbed off on me. He suspected what he had done to my prestige. Baffled and confused by their taunts, he ambled slowly from the field into the privacy of the woods, his head bowed low.

It was in the heat of that same afternoon when I slipped naked into the cool brook and swam silently in its gentle current. On the hill behind me, the ball field was empty—the game was over. Ahead lay a thick dark forest separated only by the deep winding brook. I looked for Jay, but he had disappeared somewhere in the woods to heal his wounds of embarrassment.

Why did he have to suffer so much? I had learned that the human-like God everyone worshipped had the power to heal Jay and make Mom happy. Why, then, did he choose not to? It seemed to me that Mom and Jay were yoked to a terrible fate from which they could easily be extricated. I did not understand. In human terms, it could only mean they were being punished. Isn't that what happens when loving fathers deprive their children of what they want? That was how I reasoned.

I parted the water with both arms and dove deep. Golden filaments of sunlight painted the sandy bottom with a patchwork of shifting forms. I felt The Watcher near. The water pressed against my youthful frame. A speckled trout sped from my path with a thrust of its tail. I glided through laser-like shafts of light and burst through the surface. Smells of water lilies, damp wood and fresh vegetation filled my nostrils.

I plunged into the depths again, pulling back the water until I reached the bottom and the soothing presence of The Watcher. With my foot, I pushed from a submerged boulder and sped beneath the forest's shadow. I surged upward through the metallic gray surface and gasped. There was Jay sitting forlornly on the bank. His hands clasped around his knees, he was sobbing as he rocked his forehead on his knee. I listened, undiscovered, as he complained about himself with reasons that tore at my heart.

As each precious day at home slipped past, Jay became increasingly enticed by solitude. He had given up his attempt to be what he was not in order to win my admiration. Instead, he would sit on a high limb of a particular tree in the forest and read books. From his vantage point on the forest ceiling, he would occasionally gaze out at the ball field where my friends and I played.

It was late on the last night of Jay's visit home when I woke from a sound sleep. Jay was standing in front of the bedroom window. Tears streaked down his pudgy cheeks as he watched Mom and Dad working inside the skeleton of their dream home on the knoll. I remember crawling out of bed and standing by his side. We simply stood there, looking up the hill together.

Mom stood silhouetted by a halo of yellow light from a lone bulb hanging in the rafters above her head. A bundle of boards was slung against her hip. The steady sound from Dad's handsaw blended with the symphony of cricket and frog songs that filled the night. Fireflies floated on balmy breezes that sighed through the rusted window screen. I stretched my arm across Jay's shoulders.

"I don't want to go back to that place," Jay uttered in his guttural voice. I was dumbfounded, unable to find the words to ease my brother's pain—so I just kept my eyes fixed upon the mammoth skeleton atop the knoll.

Jay suddenly bellowed, his hot breath gushing against the side of my face. "Mom, don't make me go!" His hands gripped the window sill. "Don't send me away!"

I winced. Mom turned for a moment and looked back at the darkened window of the little house. Dad reached out for a board she was carrying. Her attention came back to the task at hand. Jay slid down the wall sobbing and came to rest on the concrete floor. I took a pillow from my bed and placed it beneath his head.

He looked up at me. There was rage in his glistening eyes. Why must I go when you get to stay? his eyes seemed to ask. Why do you have the brook and the sacred woods and I have nothing, not even a home? Why do you live with my mother while I live with strangers? Why? Why? his eyes begged.

The God everyone encouraged me to worship seemed nowhere to be found unless I made him up in my mind and attached him to events. The surgeons were powerful authorities who knew so much more than I. They warned that God was watching me and listening to my every thought.

About this time, I began to be aware of the human characteristics of the God that everyone in town seemed to affirm in one way or another. At the same time, I also began to suspect that I was a disappointment to this God, to the point of incurring his anger. Inside I knew that I was far from good. In fact, I had been selfish with poor Jay for not having devoted myself to him instead of my friends. What bothered me most was that I did not love this God like his followers said they did.

I wanted to view life for what it was, but adult authorities had fastened theoretical lenses over my eyes so I would see life as they did. It no longer looked the same. When I was younger, I accepted life as it came to me, but now I found myself judging it and making it confusing. I could no longer see forever. What was left was stifled vision, where judgments and theory distorted the life I had once viewed with such clear simplicity. As I look back, it was a terrible predicament.

I suddenly felt frightened, as if I had stolen something dear to my brother and had been caught in the attempt. I pulled away and lay in bed staring down at Jay's shadow-like form on the floor. So many sorrowful emotions poured into my brain. I could not repress my thoughts. What grown-ups were teaching me about life and the way life actually impacted on me did not agree.

Confused and trying to make sense of life as I saw it through my new lenses, I reasoned that perhaps I was special. Just maybe, Jay, Mom and I had been singled out by God to carry a burden in life for some great purpose I would later discover.

The dreaded day came when Jay had to return to exile. Dad had wisely made plans to be out of town. Mom and I had breakfast in silence, while Jay remained in bed, pretending to be ill. Parents of another deaf child were coming to drive their daughter and Jay back to the institute. Sorrow clung to Mom's face that awful day as she sipped at her tea. I remember looking up at the clock on the sheetrock wall as it swept the seconds away.

Mom sighed and glanced with red eyes at the bedroom door. Like an executioner in love with the condemned, she rose up slowly to do what had to be done. I ran to Mom's bed in the next room to watch what was about to happen.

"Come on, Jay, it's time," Mom said, forming the words clearly with her lips for Jay to read.

"No, Mom. I'm sick. Please don't send me back there," he pleaded and pulled the blankets up to his neck.

She yanked the blankets off the bed. "You're not sick. Now let's g-g-go. Tha-tha-tha-tha-they'll be here any ma-ma-ma-minute."

Jay's face contorted as he begged for release from his sentence. Mom left the room, refusing to listen. I watched as he reluctantly put on his clothes. A tear slid down the side of his face as he looked up at the ceiling, complaining to some invisible friend.

A horn sounded in the driveway. His dream was over.

"Tha-tha-tha-tha-they're here."

Jay threw himself back on the bed in a wild frenzy and grabbed the metal bedpost with both hands. "No, Mom, please don't send me away."

Mom kneeled on the bed and tugged at his fingers until she pried them loose. She had begun to act a part she would probably replay in her ugliest nightmares. She finally grabbed Jay around the waist and heaved him from the bed. The bottom sheet tore against the bed springs as he crashed in a heap. I shuddered at the sound of his skull banging against the hard floor. I blinked rapidly to hold back the tears.

Like a caged animal, he jumped to his feet, knocking Mom to the floor behind him in the cramped quarters. With both hands, he braced himself against the door frame and defiantly stood his ground.

Mom lay on her side, gasping for breath, her eyes squeezed shut, not wanting to see. "Help me! Wo-wo-wo-wo-won't you please help!" she yelled at me.

Jay flinched when he saw me rise to defend Mom, but my legs refused to move against him. Alone in her struggle, Mom dragged herself to her feet. Jay's arms stiffened against the doorway as he glanced behind him at his beloved foe.

Resigned, she lowered her shoulder and careened into his back with all the force her slight frame could muster. He crashed through the doorway with a painful cry and fell onto the floor at my feet. She quickly clutched his ankles and began to drag him face down into the front room. He reached out in desperation and gripped my heel.

"Help me, please!" She gave another heave, breaking his hold. I tumbled over backwards and watched in horror as my brother's face scuffed across the worn linoleum. He had enough—there was no more fight left in him. He lay exhausted in a heap, like an animal awaiting slaughter. In his hand was a piece of linoleum, torn away in his final few feet of struggle. He pressed his face against the floor and cried.

"Okay, Mom, I'll go. I'm sorry."

She sobbed and gazed upward with a whimpering plea to a God who never seemed to listen. In a moment, she dropped to her knees by Jay's side. Years of agony gushed from her in waves as she rubbed his head in a way that soothed them both.

Jay slowly lifted himself and looked at me. He did not say a word, but there was a deep internal wound radiating pain through his glazed stare. The front of his wrinkled white shirt and navy blue pants were soiled from the ordeal. He picked up his suitcase and walked outside, leaving his dream of living with us behind. I looked into Mom's stricken face.

We watched together as a black car took Jay away. When it disappeared behind the knoll, Mom bolted to her room and slammed the door. I ran outside and sprinted down the footpath into the welcome shadows of the sacred forest and The Watcher's embrace.

I felt, at times, like there was something diabolical stalking us. I could feel its personality in the repetitive nature of the events that unfolded next.

Jay had been accepted to public school in his junior year of high school and was at last living within the family circle. We now lived in the big house on the knoll. The little house had become only a storage shed. Jay's dream had returned to him. He was in a real house instead of a dormitory, in a room he shared with a brother rather than a deaf stranger.

It seemed ironic that as Dad's business flourished, our family withered. He was not home much anymore, but when he was tension filled the air. There was also something terribly wrong between Dad and Mom. I did not know what it was, but I had a sense it was serious. As time wore on, the way I was dealing with my speech impediment was making success at school impossible; my grades were worsening and I had become a continual disappointment—a problem to my Dad.

I remember a night when I had walked the long trek home from basketball practice. I was being punished for something by Dad and had been relegated to walking home—through freezing temperatures and even snow storms from the gym. I remember how my hair would freeze into icy clumps by the time I finally arrived home. At the front door, I could hear Dad's angry shouts from inside. I thought of Jay. He was not used to Dad and was probably frightened.

I stepped into the living room. Jay was sitting hunched on a chair by the dining room table. His sweat-stained T-shirt was untucked over familiar, baggy khaki pants. Mom's back was arched protectively in front of him, her eyes glaring at Dad. She reached behind her and rubbed Jay's shoulder reassuringly. With his face flushed and his tie askew, Dad pointed his finger at Mom's face, raving about something that I can't even recall anymore.

I interceded in a way that directed Dad's anger to me. Jay read the violence in his stepfather's face and leaped up with a pathetic cry. Dad threw him aside and lunged at me. Punches landed against my chest with a sickening thud. Mom pulled at the back of Dad's collar, but he threw her onto the living room couch with a thrust from his powerful right arm. Jay ran to her side and held her back from the melee.

Dad swung from his hip and landed a jolting right on my shoulder. I plummeted over backwards into the dining room. Mom screamed. Jay kept her pinned against the couch, refusing to release her. His look told me he was not sure he was right in not coming to my aid, but Mom was his first concern. It was so much like the decision I had to make that summer morning in the little house when Jay was forced off to school.

Upright, I crouched in the corner protecting my face with my arms. Dad swarmed over me, hurling punches. Just then, a backhand I was not expecting whipped through my guard and banged against my face, slamming my head against the wall. A dull numbness buzzed at the back of my skull. Dad's eyes widened. For an instant, I saw his remorse for what had happened between us.

I shoved him aside and raced upstairs to my room. He followed me to the landing, where he pounded out his hatred against the wall. I flopped onto my bed as his tirade filled the house.

In a way I did not blame him. I was a dismal failure at school. I could only claim my self-respect in the summer on the baseball field when Dad's unique expression, wrapped around a cigar, radiated pride to me from the shadow of the dugout. And then there was his strong embrace supporting me in the brook when, as an infant, he taught me to swim and the roughness of the unshaven stubble on his face when he kissed me good night as a child.

I could not understand how such gentle love could become so embittered. I am sure Dad was as confused as I was during that awful winter. I never stopped loving him and, as I found later in life, he never stopped loving me.

Rain had turned to sleet as Dad finally stormed from the house that night. I overheard Mom making arrangements over the phone for her mother to take Jay to live with her in Connecticut.

As the night wore on, I was awakened by a sick feeling in the pit of my stomach. The room upstairs that I shared with Jay was still unfinished. There was no heat or insulation. Only roofing boards and shingles separated me from the cold winter night. Small icy stalactites hung from the shingle nails in the ceiling above my head.

My stomach lurched when I tried to crawl out of bed. Blood

that had oozed from my nose and cut lip had formed a crust on my cheek, welding a patch of hair to my pillow.

There was no time to make it downstairs so I vomited on the bare wooden floor. I thought of the illness I had bequeathed to Jay so many winters ago. The thought mixed with the stench made me sicker. On all fours, I glanced over at Jay's bed. It was empty. His alarm clock was on an old orange crate next to his bed. It was four o'clock in the morning and Grandmother should be arriving from Connecticut soon.

Just then, I heard the groan of an automobile, followed by a flash of gray light across the ceiling. In a moment, Mom's voice could be heard through the floor boards. "Oh, M-M-M-M-Mother," she sobbed. What an unhappy place the new house had become.

But my grandmother's reassuring voice brought back memories. She was a staunch Yankee who never pried into her daughter's problems and held her chin high in adversity. Her late husband had left her without financial worries in an elegant old home that matched her character. I was always solemnly respectful in her presence.

In a little while I heard the front door close. I crawled to the window and looked down to see Jay walking across the frozen front lawn behind Grandmother's steady pace. His head was bowed protectively against driving sleet.

The downcast tilt of his whole person reminded me of the time so many summer ago that he retreated from the mockery of my friends. A black suitcase hung from his hand. Everything he had in the world was stuffed inside. He stopped suddenly and looked back at Mom who was standing in the doorway. Then he turned slowly and squinted up at me. Like the rain-streaked glass, there had always been an invisible barrier separating us. He appeared withered to me, like a prisoner facing yet another sentence for a crime he never committed. He turned and marched to another black car that took him from his home and his dreams forever.

A few months later, Dad and Mom were divorced. Jay eventually became an Episcopal priest. Perhaps he had found something in the sacred woods, too.

October 22, 1991

I begin to think more about Berlyn's assassin. I find that I have developed the conviction that human beings possess a rational mind together with what I have come to call a demigod. How I see it is that our rational mind acts to keep us in accord with society and the world around us. It is as reasonable as the environment in which we live. A demigod rules us. It is, in effect, that part of our psyche that is like a God.

As I saw the murder happening, Paul's demigod rode into space and time on a wild storm of unbridled rage. In a tantrum, born of denial, it had to have smashed through the barrier of his rational mind to brutally slay Berlyn. Then, as I envisioned it, his demigod fled back into the subconscious lair from where it had come. His rational mind had followed, closing the way behind it like water filling the vacuum carved by a diving fish.

At the trial, Paul claimed that he had tripped as he entered Berlyn's room and that his gun had accidentally fired. The deputy district attorney had asked him to step down from the witness stand and demonstrate how he had tripped. Paul refused. It was then that I noticed a hint of the rage that was in my daughter's killer. His teeth clenched and his jaw tightened as the attorney asked him again. "No, you do it," Paul retorted. I felt anger begin to boil in the pit of my stomach. It was one thing to have killed Berlyn, but another to try and get away with it, I thought.

So, with Paul instructing from the witness stand, the deputy district attorney attempted to enact the stumble. From Paul's description, it seemed impossible for his gun to have discharged a bullet down into Berlyn's skull while she lay elevated on the bed. The deputy district attorney demonstrated the contortions that would had to have taken place for Paul's gun to be high enough to have fired the fatal bullet while he was falling to the floor as he had claimed. The portrayal looked absurd.

Paul also claimed that he had consumed so much alcohol that he was not in control of his actions. It occurred to me that his rational mind was repairing the breach, cause by his demigod with a variety of reasons it hoped society would find acceptable.

It seemed to me that Paul's demigod held little regard for conventional reality, the realm over which his ineffectual rational mind presided. I had the sense that Paul's demigod believed it was immortal and that his current sojourn upon the earth was of little consequence to its grand perspective.

It could be that Paul's rational mind knew nothing of why his fiendish demigod had killed Berlyn. The fiend, it seemed to me, had wrapped the reason in fear and had submerged it somewhere in its dark subconscious domain, far beyond the reach of reason.

At the trial Paul had testified that the moment after he shot Berlyn and the lights went on, he had stood there in disbelief over what had happened. I believe his rational social mind had already sealed the fiend's escape, leaving him unconnected to what it had done. He was most likely as stunned as were the spectators gathering around him. For an instant, Paul had been his savage demigod, then suddenly his reasonable self appeared and took control.

As Paul's immobility dissipated, panic rushed in to fill the void. He bolted from the room, took the elevator down to ground level and ran into the parking lot. According to Paul's testimony, he did not even know he was still carrying the gun until he looked down and noticed it in his hand. Then his rational mind collected itself enough to begin dictating orders that would protect its demigod. He hid his weapon in bushes near the hotel and fled.

I recalled testimony, Paul's amazing lack of remorse for the slaughter he had committed. Following the murder, he went home where his mother had briefly attempted to question him. According to Paul, he had simply said, "a girl was shot and they think I did it." She tried questioning him further, but he replied, "I don't want to talk about it," and went to bed.

When the police assault team arrived, they surrounded the apartment complex where Paul, his mother and two brothers lived. They cordoned off nearby streets and finally stormed into the apartment, where they had to awaken him from a sound sleep. The arresting officer had commented on how devoid of sentiment or remorse Paul had been on the long ride back to Anaheim. He never inquired into Berlyn's condition or even asked if she were alive or dead.

It occurred to me that the reason for his unemotional behavior was that Paul's rational mind could not communicate with its fiendish identity. His demigod had gone into hiding. There was simply too much to do, too much distraction for Paul's rational social mind to search for his heinous demigod now: It had to seal off the police investigation; it had to confront the furies of guilt that howled in the night; it had to protect his demigod from the media and all the while the walls of his paradigm were crashing down.

The police said Paul showed no compassion or remorse; there was no trace of a human personality. His cold, rational response was all that was left.

An untold rage smolders within me, but it is contained by two factors—my fear of being a metaphysical accomplice of Berlyn's murder, and my concept of the demigod. On a more practical note, society took Paul into its custody and away from my retribution.

October 26, 1991

It is early Saturday evening. I am in my fifteenth-floor office that overlooks the Hollywood Hills and Koreatown. I have just finished some urgent business needed for Monday and find myself exhausted.

Berlyn's portrait hangs on the wall to my left. I turn slowly to the city lights. I used to relish opportunities to impress Berlyn by taking her to memorable places and events. Now the city seems less intriguing to me. It has lost one of its enthusiastic admirers.

When Berlyn was old enough for it to have meaning, I would call her from my office and ask for a "date." I'd be sure to make it for the very same day, giving our special evening more excitement. Of course, these outings were before I had to compete with boys for her time.

Her mother would take her to the store and buy something new for the evening. Susan would fix Berlyn's hair just right and help her with her homework so the time spent together would be worry-free. I made sure to plan our dates on school nights so they would be all the more special.

One time, when Berlyn was about ten years old, I arrived home and Susan escorted me to the stairs. "Are you ready, honey?" she called up to Berlyn's room. In a few moments, our little girl appeared at the top of the stairs, grinning self-consciously. She made her way down, her hand gracefully sliding along the rail, while she forced herself not to burst out laughing.

Black patent leather shoes, feminine white socks, a blue jumper with suspenders over a white top—she was precious. She walked into my hug and wrapped her arms around my waist. I laid my cheek against the top of her head. Her long blonde hair was smooth to my touch and smelled of fresh herbal shampoo.

"You look so pretty tonight, I'm going to be the envy of everyone in the movie theater," I said as I winked at Susan.

With her little purse in hand, Berlyn skipped to the car, her waist-length hair swaying merrily behind her.

Our father-daughter dates became fewer as Berlyn grew older. Boys and basketball were taking up most of her free time. When we did go out together, I could tell she had arranged to make the time available.

She loved going into Los Angeles, to one of the more famous restaurants, where she would order something that was presented with a lot of fanfare. In her way, she was testing the world, finding out what it was all about. It was not that its opulence meant anything to her—she was just curious, wanting to experience everything.

I began to realize that my little girl was no longer "little." As we walked to our table in a downtown Los Angeles restaurant one evening, I noticed from the corner of my eye men turning to watch her pass. To me, she was simply Berlyn, now I noticed that she was being admired by strangers.

As I weaved behind her and the maitre d' through the maze of tables, it dawned on me that my little girl had entered life's play. I could no longer help her with her role; it was hers alone. I glanced around me as I sat down at our special table by the window with its view of the city. She would have to win her place with those strangers out there, I thought to myself.

She grinned across the table at me. Shimmering gold hair hung over her shoulders in stark contrast to her dark blue satin dress. Elegance was maturing through a child's veneer. Her chin was slightly raised now from the esteem she had gained for herself on the basketball court. Her sky-blue eyes were warm and kind. Berlyn had become her own person.

Already there were portions of that person that were private. I felt a small pang of pain at the thought. I supposed my regret to be the same all fathers have faced when the child they love crosses the bridge into adulthood and pauses, briefly, to look back at them.

Now she has crossed the last bridge. But unlike the one to adulthood, I can't see her play her part anymore. She has been swallowed by the darkness.

I feel myself become still inside. The presence of The Watcher emerges. The spectacular array of city lights blur together into a brilliant glow as tears fill my eyes. I sit back, close my eyes and welcome my old childhood friend. Why does The Watcher bring such relief? It is irrational, an escape from reality, but I am, nonetheless, curious about what the unique perspective The Watcher will find beyond the horizon of the self I have made.

Still, I do have mixed feelings. As bizarre as it seems, I feel hurt that The Watcher never warned me of Berlyn's pending doom. I remind myself again that The Watcher is really only a different perspective of me and can know no more than I know—or can it? I always wonder. When I was young, whatever it is that I call The Watcher often foretold events with accuracy. I feel a rush of exuberance explode within my chest.

I drift away; to the fall of the year when we had a little vacation home in a tiny hamlet on the high plains of northeastern New Mexico. For me, it was a place of escape. Morgan was an infant and Berlyn an awkward pre-teen.

I was lying in bed just before midnight. In a moment of nostalgic longing, I called The Watcher from the amber New England field of my childhood. The cackling of crows entered the silence of my mind, birds of yesteryear that had long since flown away. A spectacular winter sunset painted ice-crusted snow with fiery colors. The picture was so vivid I could even see puffs of vapor billowing from the nostrils of cows rhythmically munching hay in the distant pasture by the woods. I bathed in the mood. My old friend was rushing to me from a dark winter storm that brewed on the horizon.

Then a presence filled the room. It led me away from reality, across the field into the privacy of the sacred woods. Looking down, as I floated just above the ground I saw the rusted remains of a small shovel I had lost as a child. Camouflaged in an entanglement of briars, it was barely noticeable, but I knew it was mine and I remember the rainy autumn day when I left it there.

I never looked up at The Watcher. From the corner of my eye, I could see khaki pants in the darkness pacing beside me. They were my dad's work pants and The Watcher had my father's gait, but I never did see The Watcher.

In the woods, my bed became a piece of soft, spongy moss by the deep laughing brook that wound beneath the forest's entangled canopy. There The Watcher began to tell its story.

Oh, it was me all right; I was telling the tale and not some creature that inhabited me. That is precisely what was so wonderful about the relationship. The Watcher was a mysterious part of me that was still free.

It was more the meaning of what I was inside than the personality I had made for the world ouside. Perhaps that is why we became such intimate friends. It was wise rather than judgmental—as I had become. It was gentle while I had forced myself to become aggressive. Most important, it still carried the innocence I once had in what seemed to be so many lifetimes ago.

Here is part of what The Watcher told me as that very special night unfolded. I call it The Watcher's tale.

It began by telling me that, in the beginning, there was infinite chaos, without subject or object. Everything that ever was or is to be was in formless infinity—the disconnected stuff of reality. Suspended amidst these infinite possibilities was will. Will is the great catalyst; reactions to it create identity. Because of will, a reaction occurred that drew portions or traits of chaos together to form the first and only identity that has ever been. The subjective had erupted from the objective, the personal from the impersonal.

These traits, The Watcher explained, understood through their sheaths of mind that were continually forming so identity could know itself. In harmony with identity, mind harvested experience—the results of will—and digested its discoveries for its master.

Then mind learned rebelliousness and began to filter pure experience through judgments and concepts of its own design. Like a rogue artificial life form, it developed its own identity in secret, deep within a subconscious lair. It evolved a separate being, a demigod, knitting a resilient cocoon of reason to defend itself against absorption into the one identity.

The light that had surrounded identity's traits began to dim because its source was now outside reason's domain. Darkness descended. Suddenly, fear emerged because of what reason assumed lay beyond its limits.

In despair, the traits sent out a signal of distress; their delicate naive tremors cried through the darkness. Today, man instinctively remembers this call as music. The mournful cry drew traits together in a great swirling caldron of reality. Once identity had known only itself. Now it was one of many. The shock of this meeting began a despair that carries over to this day.

The Watcher's tale unfolded for several more hours as I lay motionless and listening. I do not know why The Watcher told me the tale or from where it had originated. At the time, I felt as though I were two people; one on one path and one on another. Every so often the paths crossed and I would meet myself as one would a stranger.

Just then I was jolted in my bed as a yellow light shot out from above my head and, for an instant, illuminated the room. I had supposed a thunderstorm was brewing outside, but the heavens were filled with stars.

As incredible and even embarrassing as it seemed to me at the time, a brazen thought occurred to me that in three days a colossal event would occur signaling the truth of The Watcher's tale. I laughed to myself for even covertly looking forward to what the third day might bring.

On the third day following this encounter, I was walking alone in the New Mexico prairie beneath more stars than I had ever before seen. It was one of those brilliant crisp nights. I had just finished reading and needed a cold refreshing wind against my face.

It was about ten o'clock when I heard horses begin to whinny and kick at the rungs of their corrals in the village behind me. Just then, coyotes in the mountains across the prairie began to howl; in unison with the faint baying of livestock in distant canyons.

I looked up sharply and froze. It appeared as if a force had stabbed the underbelly of the universe. There was just a tiny puncture directly above me but it was bleeding profusely. It was as if I were under a gigantic glass bowl turned upside down, and bright crimson poured down the inverted surface, like thick paint. I stood there, riveted by the unfolding spectacle. The village had turned a vibrant red. I could see horses leaping in the air and bucking, kicking their hind legs. The blood-red color kept pouring down from the puncture into the horizon.

I gathered myself together and ran as fast as I could toward home, sidestepping golpher holes and leaping over narrow arroyos along the way. The eerie event was passing. Dark red was turning anemic pink. Night's blackness began to return to the very center of the universe where the bleeding had first begun.

I arrived at my door out of breath, pointing for Susan and the girls to look at the night sky. The redness had all but dissipated. Susan related that a news bulletin had just appeared on television reporting a magnetic disturbance in the atmosphere that had caused a phenomenon similar to the northern lights.

The girls in their nightgowns stood with me on the porch and watched as the last vestiges of the event, a vibrant pink haze, disintegrated into darkness. In a few moments, the disturbance was over, and with it, all traces of The Watcher's prediction. What did remain was a deepening sense of intimacy with my old companion.

The girls were too excited to go back to bed. The night was too magical. We gathered up their sleeping bags, threw them into the old flat-bed truck by the side of the house and drove just a few hundred yards down the steep, rocky incline to a sandy cove on the shore of Ute Lake.

It was not long before Berlyn and Morgan were sleeping soundly their faces illumined by an umbrella of shifting amber light from our campfire. Bubbling blobs of charred marshmallows that had fallen from their roasting sticks clung to the stones that encircled the burning embers. Dried mesquite hissed and popped in the flames, sending orange sparks spiraling skyward into darkness.

Susan sat next to me on a flat boulder and poked at the fire with her roasting stick. Without looking up she asked, "What did you learn the other night—from your Watcher, I mean?" Her voice was trusting and contented. There was no brooding trouble behind her words or inner wounds that were distracting her in those wonderful days when Berlyn was a little girl.

I suddenly felt uncomfortable. Putting the experience into words made it seem irrational, to the point of being bizarre. I feared she would regard my experience as preposterous, especially in view of her Hispanic heritage, in which anything that deviates from strict Catholic theology is considered heretical.

She looked up at me. "Tell me about it." Her dark eyes

reverted to their fascination with the fire. Her tone conveyed a naive acceptance of whatever The Watcher was about.

I looked up at the star-studded arch of the Milky Way at the same time as a satellite traversed the heavens. I can still see Berlyn rolling over onto her back at that moment and drawing in a deep breath, her sleeping bag pulled up under her chin. Morgan had cuddled up against her with her head tucked into the nape of Berlyn's neck.

The vast lake lay smooth that night, mirroring the stars, as it stretched to the cliffs of the distant shore. I led Susan to the water's edge. We stood there together before a sparkling blanket of starlight that covered the ink-black depths as I recounted The Watcher's tale. A fish had leaped up and dropped back into the pitch-like blackness with a sharp plunking sound. Ever-widening ripples raced outward, causing reflections of stars to bob and weave. We looked up. The satellite had returned, climbing the heavens once again.

November 1, 1991

Today Paul is sentenced. I sit in my usual courtroom seat. The plump, middle-aged judge focuses his eyes on the prosecutor. Never once looking directly at Paul, except for the occasional glance from the corner of his eye, he calmly issues a prison term of nineteen years to life.

Paul looks down at his folded hands for a moment, then signs an appeal that his attorney pushes in front of him. In a moment, the bailiff comes to the defendant's table, handcuffs Paul and leads him away. The last I see of my daughter's murderer is when he exits through the side rear door of the courtroom. On his way out, he glares up at the ceiling, his face is covered with the look of shocked disbelief for what has happened to his life.

November 2, 1991 - Los Angeles Times by Mark Pinsky:

Paul————, *a 19-year-old dropout convicted of second degree murder . . . was sentenced Friday to 19 years to life in prison. . . . The sentence was just a year short of the maximum allowed by law, attorneys said.*

Judge Theodore E. Millard sentenced him to 15 years to life on the second-degree murder conviction, as required by law. He also added 4 years—of a maximum 5—for using a weapon, a .357 magnum pistol, in the shooting.

Despite pleas from [Paul's] defense attorney . . . Millard ordered that the sentences be served consecutively, meaning that he will not be eligible for parole for 12 years.

The judge also refused a request from the defense to allow [Paul] to serve part of his sentence in the California Youth Authority. . . . Instead, Millard ordered that [he] be sent to the state prison at Chino.

Glendale News Press

Orange County Superior Court Judge Theodore Millard called the case a "true tragedy" and said [the] 19-year-gold defendant . . . was "a time bomb ready to go off, unfortunately he went off that morning."

[Paul] . . . dressed in an orange jail jump suit and tennis shoes, didn't show any emotion during the sentences.

November 9, 1991

I sit next to Morgan in the Rose Bowl about halfway up in the stands behind the north goal post. She won tickets to the UCLA football game for her outstanding performance in a youth league basketball clinic earlier that day. She is excited at the opportunity of treating me to an evening she thought I would enjoy. A bright full moon hangs low on the eastern horizon, the crisp autumn air smells of change. The stands are like steep cliffs awash with vibrant colors, the stadium floor an island of deep green.

On the way to the bowl, Morgan had told me about a dream she had had the night before. I had intended to think more about The Watcher's tale this night. What presses against my thoughts now is Morgan's dream. There has been no rest from her unraveling that began with Berlyn's death. White water is everywhere.

Morgan's dream began with a visit by one of her girl friends. According to Morgan, her friend stood before her smiling. "Then her face changed. It turned into the face of my friend, Jason," Morgan recounted with a worried tone. "Jason?" she had asked the specter in her dream. "He started laughing. As soon as he did, he changed into my other friend, Tracy. It was awful, Dad. I ran into the front yard to get away from them. That's when I came upon this long black limousine."

"A limo?"

"Maybe it was a hearse; I don't know, but there was this tall guy with a long face standing beside it. 'I'll take you,' he said to me. 'No,' I said. 'I'll stay here.'"

"Good answer," I said.

"Then the man said, 'You asked to go, so now you have to.'"

"Wow, honey, that does sound scary," I said, concerned.

"Yeah, I know. I sat in the back seat, huddled in the corner while he drove me away. After a while, he stopped and I climbed out. He drove off. I was in New Mexico, standing there by the side of this deserted road. The wind was blowing pretty hard."

She placed her hands over her face, then drew them down, pulling at her lower eyelids and lips. The color had drained from her cheeks. I felt helpless in trying to comfort her. I feared her dream was one of many that were awaiting her. Paul's face flashed before me.

"Then, I looked up the road to the top of a hill," she continued. "There was a lady up there. Behind her it was night and there was a forest. In front of her it was desert and day. She had long blond hair that blew across her face. She said, 'I know the way.'

"I walked up the hill to where she was. I knew it was Berlyn. I just knew it was Berlyn, but I couldn't see her face. She took me to the side of the road where she spread a bush apart with her hands. I stepped through the space and I found myself home, at our front door. It was Berlyn, Dad. She showed me the way home." I feel a snap of pain in my heart.

Shouts from a passing peanut vendor interrupt my thoughts. I stand up and call out, "Hey, peanuts, here." The vendor, a college student or perhaps a little older, reaches into the big box strapped around his neck and hands me a couple of small bags. He is tall, his pale face glistens in the harsh stadium lights. His shirt is drenched and curly wet hair lies matted against his temples. He wears a baseball cap and glasses with thick lenses that are speckled with beads of sweat.

"You know," I begin as I pay him and sit down, "I always wondered how much you fellows earn selling a bag of peanuts." Suddenly, he begins to grimace, his lips wrench together and his eyes squeeze shut. Struggling to answer, he cannot force out even a single word. The young man is a stutterer. Finally, a sound, a fragment of a syllable, escapes his lips. His eyes open and he glances at the people who are staring at him. He stands there in desperation, spewing bits of sound. Behind his panicky eyes and tense muscles, I know well the inner voice of hysteria that is exploding in his brain.

"Hey, peanuts," an overweight man with a black mustache shouts impatiently a few rows farther down as he waves a couple of dollars high above his head. The vendor turns, glances back at me with a forced smile, then ambles down the steps.

Morgan looks up at me. I can tell she is studying my expression as I watch the vendor wade into the colorful throng several sections away.

My thoughts turn to the week following one Christmas, in what seemed another age:

I had just arrived by train at the small university in northern New Mexico, where I had been accepted on academic probation.

I had left a college in Minnesota six months before because the academic dean there had demanded I take speech and a foreign language in order to be on a track toward graduation. After leaving school, I went to Europe for a while where I worked my way around the continent, doing hard manual labor. My sojourn in Europe was a way of rebelling.

When I returned home, I went to the library of my New England hometown, where I browsed through stacks of college catalogues. I was looking for a university where speech and a foreign language were optional. As it turned out, there was one, and it was located in northern New Mexico.

I had stowed my belongings in my dorm room. I was the only person in the building; everyone else was at home for the holidays. The mountain air was biting cold as I stepped outside to case the campus. Only a faint pink haze remained from the setting sun, outlining the Sangre De Cristo Mountains to the north. There was the crunch of ice-crusted snow beneath my shoes. I noticed a lone lighted window in the administration building and ventured inside.

My footsteps echoed in the marble corridors as I walked down a darkening hall into the light that streamed through an open door. I looked inside. A tired-looking, rather large woman sat behind a desk in a small cramped office. She looked up at me over her reading glasses. Her lips were painted red, and her graying hair was pulled back in a bun with loose strands hanging in disarray by the sides of her face.

She smiled warmly. "Well, you're here early. Welcome. I'm Professor Gibbens."

I unfastened my long trench coat as I tried to pronounce my

name. From the corner of my eye, I noticed her smile fade away for a moment, then resurface. I stuttered severely. There were no words I could substitute—my name was my name.

As I sat there in front of her desk, she asked me questions that I could answer with a word or two in between sips of cocoa we shared from her thermos. It occurred to me that the time had come to strike the bargain the rest of my education would depend upon. I could not be a successful student if I were on the run; that much I had learned.

It took me quite a while, but in the end, I explained my dilemma. I told her that all indications pointed to the fact that I was not university material, but I still had a desire to learn. My education so far had been a horrifying experience.

I asked if she would allow me to be silent in her classes and hand in written rather than oral work. Then, if I continued to flounder academically, I would leave and never return.

The old professor placed her elbows on the desk and leaned toward me, staring straight into my eyes. "Mark," she said in a determined voice, "in my classes you will never have to do anything you don't want to do." I felt a tremendous weight lift from my chest.

She leaned back against her chair and thumped her fist on the desk. "And, I will see to it that professors in my department follow suit." A warm smile returned to her face. She had just orchestrated the happiest day of my life and she was delighted too.

"What do you teach?" I asked through an excited grin.

"Philosophy. I'm chairman of the department."

Because of my stuttering I had suddenly become a philosophy major in a little university high in the mountains of northern New Mexico. If she had been a physics professor, I would have become a physicist—it did not matter. All that was important to me in those calamitous days of my youth was to avoid stuttering and have an opportunity to learn along side my peers. I did not know it then, but in a few short years I would graduate with honors.

Just then, the crowd surges as UCLA kicks a field goal. A roar saturates the night air. I strain to keep sight of the peanut vendor, but I have lost him in the crowd's sudden rise. All that remains of our brief encounter is the empathy I felt for him.

November 10, 1991

With Paul's sentencing completed, reporters and their camera crews migrate off in search of other stories. Local newspapers no longer carry front-page headlines and photos about Berlyn. It is odd, but along with the sudden relief, there is an accompanying sense of regret that the proceedings are over. It means another chapter in Berlyn's life, however awful, has drawn to a close and soon there will be nothing left of us. It is like closing the casket all over again. Parts of her life are being finalized forever. Girls with whom she had played basketball and boys she had befriended visit from time to time, but the phone does not ring much anymore. Her friends have gone off to colleges and universities across America. In a very short time, they will become adults and begin families of their own, but Berlyn will remain seventeen forever.

I shake off the thought and turn my attention to The Watcher. A warm wind comes from out of the sun and sighs through a nearby pine. I survey the canyon from my nest high up in the Angeles Forest.

I used to feel self-conscious about my other perspective as The Watcher until I became involved with actors and saw how such thinking was practically applied. I remember being with Jerry Lewis when he critiqued one of his performances by saying, in effect, Jerry should have done this or Jerry should have done that. It seemed to me that he spoke to his renowned character as if it were a separate personality.

Hugh Krampi became the very popular actor, Hugh O'Brian, known best for his portrayal of Wyatt Earp in television's earlier days. In working with the "Hughs," I found that Hugh O'Brian came with a demeanor and lifestyle that Hugh Krampi often projected as a means to an end. I discovered that projected personalities were commonplace. It seemed to me that some people used them quite successfully to answer a personal need and to obtain what they wanted.

My heart suddenly throbs with loneliness. I smell a hint of the sea in the breeze that rushes against me. A sea gull hangs motionless in the air, toying with a unique balance between gravity and thermal currents that push upward from the canyon floor.

I recall another time when I had sought out The Watcher. I had just finished a job interview with a company in Boston in which I had stuttered severely, making a shambles of the whole ordeal. I recall how the interviewer shook his head and sighed, "I'm sorry but this job is just not suited to you." I felt terrible. Susan was counting on me. I could not bear to see the disappointment in her eyes again. There had been other interviews with the same results.

Once outside my face tightened at the first touch of cold air. I buttoned my coat against the damp chill and walked aimlessly through the redstone industrial complex for an hour or so, waiting for Susan to arrive. I glanced into windows at executives who were busy brooding over papers inside their warm offices. I felt apart. Sleet began to pelt down. I bowed my head as I trudged along, much as Jay had the night he left home.

The solace I felt on migrating to my other viewpoint that day—that of The Watcher—was comforting. There I found welcome compassion for the self I had made who seemed unable to win. The Watcher's lair was a safe haven where I could reflect upon what was happening to me. I guess it became what the sacred woods had been in the days of my youth.

As I walked off my embarrassment, I thought of how God and evil seemed to me to be connected somehow. God was still the strict unyielding father who continually chastised me with what I feared most—stuttering. He was still in control. Taking what I had been taught literally, what else could my ordeal have been but divine punishment? What have I done? I asked myself. Then, there was Jay's ordeal, and Mom's. It occurs to me that I had projected my concept of God onto life and now it was reflecting what was in me rather than what was real.

December 22, 1991

We are spending the holidays with Susan's family in northern New Mexico on the border of the Navajo reservation. Both Susan and Morgan need the support of familiar customs and faces. I simply need to be alone.

I lean against the kitchen door frame and watch Susan and her older sister preparing green chile stew. She is happy again. As soon as the pilot of our plane had announced that we were entering New Mexico's skies, I turned and saw her expression brighten. Outside the steam-coated window above the kitchen sink, icicles have turned orange in the waning light of the setting sun. "Are you going back into the canyon?" Susan asks as she whips a tortilla from the stove and slaps another down in its place.

"Would it be okay with everyone?" I ask almost apologetically, fastening the top button of my jacket.

"It's fine. I know you need to go. Just don't stay too late like last night. We were worried." She turns and begins conversing with her sister in Spanish. They are laughing together and it is good to see.

I step outside. Crusted snow snaps beneath my shoes. Shoving my hands in my pockets, I trudge up the dirt road that leads out of the village and into, what is for me, another world. I slither through a barbed-wire fence and climb a steep hill onto the rim of a broad canyon.

The village is silent far below. Susan's family has always been kind to me I think, looking back. They are good people, hard working, with traditions that are as strong as they are warm. They have graciously freed me from any social guilt that would have otherwise resulted from my long absences on extended forays into the canyon. Berlyn would have adored Christmas in the mountains with her grandparents.

The crisp air is sweet and laden with the scent of burning mesquite from wood-burning stoves in the village. Coyotes begin wailing from the mountains deep in the Indian lands as the last of a bright red sun disappears behind the silhouette of a distant mesa; the sky is ablaze with fiery clouds that resemble dying embers.

I have no direction. No humans can help me. The further I wander from my old paradigm in search of the origins of god, evil and fear, the more suspicious I become that life itself might be the only real entity that exists—the one all-encompassing creature. All other interpretations of existence seem born from my own shallow judgments that I project onto events.

Many years ago when I was very young, The Watcher once conveyed the idea to me that it was life and I was the living. I live in the life. I never really knew what that idea meant until now.

In my journey I am finding early pioneers of monotheism to be correct in their assumption. They had found one essence as the basis for everything. Then, it seems to me, they projected a human personality onto their assumption, making a god through whom they could bargain with life.

I found that in those early minutes of our existence, wind and rain, mountains and fire took on human intentions. Even animals of the forest, birds and fish were attributed human traits befitting their instinctive natures. Life became a drama in which everything played a supportive role to the humans. It occurred to me that reality may lay hidden beneath the human personality I had learned to aggrandize as god.

I recall how at times since Berlyn's murder being alone has become frightening. A friend of mine once arrived home to find that he had been burglarized. He told me how on walking into his disheveled living room he had felt violated by a "sinister force."

Berlyn's murder unleashed a barrage of similar sensations in me, even to the extent of skewing my vision to see only that for which I was on continual alert. I would constantly draw together what would seem to be unrelated occurrences, but their combination would mold reality into what I feared most. I do not know why my reason tortures me in such a way, but it seems attracted to whatever frightens me.

Irrational as it may seem, I also fear being shot in the head by some crazed human lurking in the shadows. Even out here in the wilds, I find myself continually glancing over my shoulder into the darkness behind me. My world has become a very scary place. I force myself to wade through these reflex reactions to Berlyn's murder, but it is difficult and draining.

I begin to think more about fear. I wanted to simply convene with nature and to be at peace for just a few moments, but life and the moods it unleashes will not be so scheduled. The need to examine fear has surfaced and there is no turning away. I am unable to focus on a particular reason for the sudden train of thought; it simply arrives and will not yield.

I turn from the fiery western horizon to face the darkening Indian lands. I pick off the top of a sage brush, crush it between my fingers and smell its deep rustic scent. The canyon grows silent as the coyotes begin their nightly hunt. A bright moon hangs just above the far wall of the canyon, a piñon bush casting a long, dark shadow against it.

I recall my childhood home and the sacred forest. During the day, the forest had been my haven, a wondrous, colorful world in which I chased after imagination. I knew the forest and it knew me. The brook that meandered through its cool shadows caressed me with a cold embrace on hot August days. When I became tired, the sacred forest cradled me in a soft bed of moss and fern. From The Watcher's perspective, I now remembered what I thought I had forgotten long ago.

Frogs, birds and all manner of living creatures would welcome me with joyous cries when I entered their domain to be with them. "He is here! Here he comes!" they screeched and squawked to one another. I picture myself as a little boy entering the sacred forest. Even the breeze would swoop down to welcome me, awakening leaves on the trees to applaud my arrival.

Then, night descended. Fireflies would dart through the black air. As the night darkened, something terrible would happen to the forest. I remember standing in the knee-high grass of the field next to our house, gazing warily at the darkened perimeter of the woods.

Like adults whose nocturnal activities are kept hidden from the eyes of children, the personality of the forest would suddenly change with the advent of darkness. It was no longer the forest I knew. With the night, it became a demon's lair. Its welcome had withdrawn behind a barrier of menace. The sacred woods and all its creatures had become prisoners of the night. Why does the darkness change my forest? I asked myself.

It has been many years since I have played in the sacred forest. I am sure all its creatures who once knew me have gone, but I am also sure that darkness still falls and with it the ancient menace I once knew. Still, after all these years, the question remains: Why did the darkness change my forest?

I came to a fallen, sun-bleached log that juts out from a snow drift. I sit down and lean back against a thick branch. As starlight begins to speckle the heavens, the sound of feathered wings whip the air overhead.

For me, fear is being in jeopardy, not having control—chaos. It also seems to me that by attaching special significance to what I fear, I plant the seeds for the abstract concept of evil. In such a way, my childhood fear of stuttering created much of the foundation for my concept of evil, which religious teachings would reinforce.

It also occurred to me that what I feared became what I judged to be evil. For me, evil became the offspring of fear, one breathing life into the other. I never thought to question the process until, in my mind, I had somehow caused Berlyn's murder.

Furthermore, my confirmation of the existence of evil was assured because it was actually my own projection. A projected evil personality has intimate knowledge of its host's greatest fear because it *is* its host's greatest fear. Therein, I believe, lies the power of evil.

December 25, 1991

I sit in the darkened church at the end of a long pew occupied by Susan's relatives. Subtle, dim lights inside silver vases hang along the walls. We are at midnight mass, and going to it is a tradition in Susan's family. Outside, the temperature is well below freezing, the night sky a star-studded arch that cradles the little village.

The priest with altar boys and dignitaries from the Catholic community are lined up in the entryway, awaiting the choir in the loft behind me to herald their entrance. It is the first time I have been in the church in sixteen years. The only other occasion was funeral services for Susan's brother-in-law, who had drowned.

Rows of lamps hanging down from the high ceiling are suddenly illuminated. I glance up casually and then freeze. The dots of light I had seen last July—there they are again—shining through the decorated metal that wraps the glass bowl of the lamps. I gasp and steady myself against the pew in front of me.

I think back to that dark, early summer morning, when I had been awakened by a strange awareness—the bright dots, forming a pattern that resembled infant sprouts of corn. The balls of lights that had sprayed up from below the foot of my bed had now been perfectly replicated in the lamps. My eyes well up, blurring the soft white dots.

Had Berlyn communicated with me that night? Was time so irrelevant then that I was already where I am now? I feel grateful, ecstatic and toyed with all at the same time.

Perhaps a form of communication has been passed to me, I think, to which I cannot respond. I do not know how. Maybe my species has not evolved far enough to translate the experience. It is like trying to communicate through a one-way mirror. The frustration is unbearable.

1992

The silver and red passenger jet ascends into the New Mexico sky, streaking through wisps of morning clouds. Susan lies back against the seat beside me and closes her eyes. Morgan leans forward and grins from her window seat as she feels the powerful thrusts of the engines. I wink at her.

I pull a book of ancient myths from my briefcase and begin to read. After a short while, I look up, thinking something through, and I glance out the window to watch the steep cliffs of the Pecos wilderness drift slowly beneath the wing.

The scene reminds me of an October day in the Pecos wilderness after Susan and I had left New England and returned to New Mexico. I had finally landed a job as a fund raiser, of all things, for a national health organization. My territory covered all of New Mexico and west Texas. The interview had gone well.

Out of sheer necessity I was beginning to master one-on-one conversations and it helped that my boss had been kind and made me feel comfortable. It also helped that the organization was desperate, needing someone right away who would work for relatively low pay and be eager about developing such a large territory alone.

I had to chuckle after telling my new boss I would take the job. He looked at me with disbelief, saying, "You mean you want it? How are you and your wife going to live on the pay?"

None of that mattered to me. It was the only position I had found that offered me a chance to compete. The job had chosen me—no one else wanted it. My life had suddenly taken a new direction, channeled as it was by another decision born from circumstance rather than desire. But that was okay. It gave Susan and me what we needed—at least, for today.

As it turned out, my boss' office was in Denver, so I was pretty much on my own. If my stuttering caused me to fall down on the job, I could get up by myself and no one in the organization would know. It meant I would essentially have control. I had been with the organization for more than a year and had already won a promotion, along with two national honors.

My work in raising funds for the needy began, in a way, like a game I used to play as a kid in the sacred forest. I'd jump from stump to stump across a swamp. With the stuttering in close pursuit, I could easily slip and fall in the mud and skunk cabbage. Now I would awaken with the question, "Will they catch me today?" and go to bed with the thought, "I made it one more time."

What helped me most in my work, in spite of my impediment, was sincerity. It gave me a leg up over my speech impediment. When I first began my career with the Muscular Dystrophy Association, I considered myself the representative of dying children. So when I walked into some corporate leader's office for a meeting, I came bearing the hopes and suffering of very sick youngsters. I was bringing this very busy person a chance to do something wonderful.

I was providing the opportunity to share in the lives of the most courageous children in the world. I no longer mattered; only the kids did.

When I was, say, in a comfortable lobby, awaiting an appointment with someone very rich and powerful, I would think about the children who were counting on me. I would recall their personalities until they became more powerful and important to me than the tycoon I was about to visit.

I remember one time when I was waiting to see a very popular and busy movie star who was continually catered to. He was a man to whom everyone always said "yes." While waiting in his lobby, I recalled summer camp with the children. Camp was not something I was required to attend, but I did because it was where the children gave me my zeal. In a way, they commissioned me there. Without them I was nothing.

The counselors and I used to make rounds at night to the different cabins where we'd turn the kids over in their beds since they did not have the strength to turn themselves. I remember rolling a twelve-year-old pudgy little boy onto his side. His name was Milton. "Turn my pillow over, will ya?" he asked of me. His arm hung lifelessly across his round tummy. I pulled his other arm out from under him. He grinned when I placed his head on the cool side of the pillow. "Boy, am I glad you came in," he said. "I had a mosquito biting my face all night."

Milton had come from a tragically poor home. His father was a roughneck on an oil rig in southern New Mexico—when he was sober; his mother, a big strapping woman with a dirty-faced brood that clung to her skirt. One day, Milton's sister was pushing him in his wheelchair in the vacant lot by their shanty when she hit a rut. Milton spilled out onto the ground and broke his leg. I went to see him in the hospital. His broad smile greeted me as I entered the room. I held his hand. "Don't worry," he said in a slow southern drawl, as if consoling me. "I'll make it to summer camp. Don't you worry about that. I'll be there."

A few months later, the cast was removed from his leg. Then, as he endured the pain of physical therapy to make himself ready for camp, something else went wrong. The therapist broke the brittle bones of Milton's atrophied ankle. He lay for months in his bedroom, in front of an old black-and-white television, immersed in depression. Still, he refused to give in. He kept his promise to me that year and healed in time for summer camp at Ghost Ranch in northern New Mexico. He renewed acquaintances with all his friends who, like him, were dying.

I recalled the things we did together that week—how I held him in the saddle atop a gentle horse that walked lazily around a corral, threw his fishing line in the pond and reeled it back when the red-and-white bobber ducked beneath the surface. We had stocked the little mud hole with so many fish for the kids that they were bumping into each other! Kids like Milton never demanded much from life, a cool side of a pillow, a ride on a horse, catching a fish—not much at all.

At week's end, a volunteer squadron of private planes took Milton and the rest of our campers home. I remember carrying him down the wing of the plane and placing him back in his wheelchair. One of his sisters pushed him across the runway to where his worn-out mother waited. He never looked back at me that day. His head hung down, his once-happy face wore a scowl. Only poverty and old television shows awaited him. He would lie in a soiled bed, looking out the window at kids playing in the field next door. A few months later, I learned that Milton had died. There is an iron marker on the prairie that catches an occasional tumbleweed marking the place where one of the human family's bravest sons is buried.

Milton and kids like him have made me successful. Their

goodness accompanied me into the meeting rooms of the most powerful. It was their suffering that bought me precious time with people who could help. I was not a super salesman or manipulator. It was what Milton and his friends had been through that caused them to listen—not me.

When I was finally summoned into the celebrity's inner sanctum, I found him sitting at a broad table, flanked on either side by an entourage of men and women who I could tell were untouched by Milton. They only wanted to please the actor, to do what he wanted done for his career, to sell the products he promoted. They would tolerate me only as long as their boss remained in charge.

I began outlining the project I had in mind, using my fluency skills to the max. There were hot stares from every angle. Then I looked into the screen hero's eyes and told him about Milton and his friends whom I represented. I explained from my heart how much these little ones needed his help. Something began to happen to his expression; it softened.

A women executive in the group interrupted with a demand for something—I can't recall now what it was now. The celebrity watched to see how I handled her. In a way, I guess I let Milton answer. She looked back down to her notebook and wrote something. The actor paused for a moment looking hard at me as he swiveled back and forth in his chair. "Okay, let's do it," he said. The rest of the group nodded their approval.

In spite of the popular notion that the wealthy and powerful are always selfish misers, I find many of them to be the most giving. Second to them are the poor themselves, many of whom are born in the crucible of despair. Suffering is a close relative to many of them, so they often help as much as they can. Social activists, the people among us who scold society for its cruelties, people I had assumed would be the most generous, turned out to be the least helpful, demanding instead that the rich do it for them.

The wing slices through a ragged white cloud. I recall an old farm truck that had lumbered over a two-tire track path somewhere in the Pecos wilderness far below:

A bearded farmer, slight of build, bounced up and down in his seat, his narrow, pointed chin angled up, as he strained to see over the steering wheel. It was late autumn. We growled up a steep incline, clinging to the side of a cliff. The wild Chama River lay twisted on the canyon floor like a long gray ribbon. I watched as an eagle soared beneath me, scanning the dark shadows. A gigantic fireball hung just above the edge of the world, immersing jagged peaks in spun gold haze.

We drove for miles down into the canyon, first through fiery aspen groves, then up onto flat barren mesas. Rounding a bend, the old truck squealed to a halt. "There it is—the monastery." I climbed down from the truck and stood there with my duffle bag in hand as the farmer turned the truck around and bounced down the road.

I had come to spend my two weeks vacation in silence, with Trappist brothers, while Susan visited with her family. I was not even Catholic. I did not know what was driving me, perhaps that other path, the one The Watcher walked had again crossed with mine. I could feel the yearning to be there. It was like coming home.

Inside, I knew that this path, the one that wound away from everything I knew and trusted, was the only one worth taking. All the others seemed to me to lead to what I called "busi-ness," keeping busy until life was over. No, for me, there was no possible substitute for this solitary adventure. It is how, in those days, I approached what I felt lay behind the obvious. Nothing else equaled the passion I had. To me, the search for the ineffable was my hidden purpose in life.

I noticed to my left a single-story adobe nestled behind a group of boulders, its mud bricks blending perfectly into the terrain. A hand-painted wooden sign stood in purple sage nearby: "Guest House."

Constructed in an L-shaped design, the building enclosed a well-kept courtyard on two sides. In the center was a rough-hewn log statue of Saint Benedict, its natural limbs forming the saint's outstretched arms. A woodpecker peered out from a nook hollowed in the statue's chest and tilted its head as I approached.

A hill sloped down from the guest house to a flat, cultivated field; the Chama rushed along its banks, paralleling the massive cliffs behind me. Looking northward into the dark canyon, I noticed a chapel spire and an adjoining convento on a hill about two hundred yards away. A small cluster of adobe cells lay nestled behind the chapel against the cliff wall.

Just then, the orange glow of a kerosene lantern emerged from the farthest door of the guest house, swinging back and forth to the rhythm of heavy boots smacking against the rocky courtyard. In a few moments, the approaching shadow melted into the darkness and a monk appeared beneath a blue hooded tunic. As the stranger raised the lantern to his shoulders, light suffused his face, revealing a long scar across his nose and down his cheek. Curly hair crept out from beneath his hood. His welcoming smile eased my apprehension.

"Greetings. I'm Father Marcos," he began, his dark deep set eyes studying my face. "Here, let me take your bag." He hoisted my duffle bag over his shoulder with a groan and motioned for me to follow. As he showed me to my room, his lantern shed a dim, orange circle around our feet. Father Marcos was average in height, about forty years old—the abbot of the enclave, presiding over four other monks who live in the remote outpost. What I noticed most about him was the remnant of an inscrutable smile that played on his lips.

My simple eight-by-nine-foot cell overlooked the Chama. It had a fireplace sculpted from the adobe wall, a mattress on an adobe slab and a wooden desk with a lantern on top. After wishing him goodnight, I lay down on the rudimentary bed and looked out the open door at a brilliant silver moon rising up above the cliffs. Coyotes began to yelp and cry from distant hills, joining the monotone symphony of the rushing Chama.

On my third day there, I had chopped wood for the community all morning. In the late afternoon, I rested on a white flat rock that had been made warm by the afternoon sun. It sat in the shallows of the Chama River about twenty feet from shore. The chaotic rhythm of the rapids relaxed me. A warm breeze rushed up the river and caressed my face. A flurry of red and orange leaves hovered down into the current and were carried away.

I sensed The Watcher was near. The feeling reminded me of The Watcher's tale and how mind's true function was simply to harvest and understand experience for identity. I remember I lay there for hours, trying to detach myself from the filters my reason had invented, through which all experience had to flow. I tried to pull my mind back from in front of me, to anchor it behind my eyes as a receptor. In the only way I knew, I was trying to adjust millenniums of evolution and make my mind a harvester again. The Watcher was so close I could all but feel it breathing as me. The separated paths of my life were coming together again.

I study my reflection in the window of the plane wondering how I could have been so foolishly naive. I recall what happened next that day in the river. It is an occurence that still has me perplexed.

Suddenly, as I lay on the rock, The Watcher whispered, "There's a fish over there by the big rock. Tell the fisherman."

My eyes flicked open. I quickly raised up on my elbows and looked over at a huge boulder protruding from the river about twenty yards upstream. "What fisherman?" I remember asking myself outloud. Just then, I heard a rustling in the forest behind me. A tall lanky man in hip boots, a flannel coat and a cowboy hat stumbled out onto the river bank. He shook his head disgustedly at his tangled line and ripped his empty fish basket from the clutches of a briar bush. "There's a fish by the big rock," The Watcher repeated. "Tell the fisherman."

"Hi," I said. He looked up at me with a start, realizing he was on private property and probably suspecting I was one of the Trappist brothers.

"Howdy," he replied. "I hope I'm not in the way here, but I ain't caught noth'n all day. No one I've talked to up and down the river has caught a thing. So, I figure I'll just hike my way upstream a ways and try my luck. I'll be on my way shortly as soon as I get this tangle out," he said, fumbling with his fishing reel. "There, that's got it."

"See that big rock over there?" I asked, feeling like a jerk.

"Yeah," he answered.

"Well if you cast your line over there, you'll catch a fish." There, I did it, I thought to myself as I felt redness spill into my cheeks.

For some reason, the stranger did not say a word. He simply did what I had told him to do as if he were mechanically obeying an unquestionable mandate. He turned like an automaton to face the rock and cast his line. No sooner had his line hit the water than a huge rainbow trout jumped into the air with the fisherman's lure dangling from the corner of its mouth.

"Ya-hoo," the cowboy shrieked. "This is the biggest fish I've ever seen in these parts! Holy smokes, look at that bugger jump!" I felt a chill up my back.

I still do not know what to make of what happened in the river that day.

My thoughts return to the monastery. I remember it was dusk when I left the Chama and ventured up onto the high mesa to help bring home the sheep. Following the long climb, I sat for a moment, my back resting against a boulder. Red and purple embers of a dying sun were scattered across the pale horizon. My rough dungaree jacket held distinctive smells of wool, pine and sage. I rubbed the stubble on my unshaven face with my hands that now had callouses on them and I realized that the tense furrows in my forehead had almost disappeared.

I kept thinking about the fisherman and my experience in the river. I tucked the thoughts away to think about later. How I loved the silence of the monastery. I guess it is the reason I went there as often as I could. I certainly did not go for the ceremonial religion and all its rites of passage. For me it was the only place where I could be silent and follow my own path.

I could see Malcolm, the old collie that lived with the community, peering over the sagebrush from the steep path. Shyly, he sauntered over and lay down by my side with a groan, dropping his head on my lap. He glanced up at me with guilty eyes, as if asking permission after the fact. Malcolm's ears twitched.

Just then, Father Marcos appeared on the mesa and nodded his greeting. He stood for a moment gazing out over the canyon, catching his breath. Malcolm sighed and rolled over on his side so I could scratch his chest. "How are you?" the father asked, lifting the rule of silence.

I nodded.

"You sure chopped a lot of wood for us this morning. I can't remember when our stockpile has been so high. Thank you." He sat down in the shade of a sprawling piñon bush, wiped his brow and pulled a stack of letters from his tunic. "Look," he said with a tired sigh. "All I want to do is be a simple monk and they make me abbot with so many worldly concerns I must attend to."

I asked him about the rule of silence of which I had become so fond. "Why do Trappist brothers practice it?"

My question took him by surprise. He had to think for a moment. "I can best explain it to you the way a wise old abbot once explained it to me," he began, looking out over the landscape below the mesa's edge. "I was a young novice then and I was with the abbot in his garden." He smiled—a wide, full smile. "Oh, how he loved his garden. I don't know why. He could never see what he planted come to life. My abbot was blind. I remember asking him about the rule. He smiled and said, 'My son, I can give you nothing because I have nothing. Not even the shoes on my poor feet are mine.'

"Just then, I remember, the bells rang for noonday prayer. I had never heard them so crystal clear as on that day. My abbot paused for a moment and chuckled to himself at the infallible timing. 'Listen,' he said to me, 'the one thing I have which I can give you is my silence. Silence to listen.'"

The bells atop the chapel's tall spire resounded through the canyon. Father Marcos looked skyward and laughed. "Time to bring in the sheep and get ready for vespers."

The plane bounces on a thermal current, bringing me back to the present. We are passing over the Grand Canyon. Once I stood on its rim with my arm draped across Berlyn's shoulders. Showing her the world had been a joy.

Susan wakens from a sound sleep and tries to smile at me, but I can already see the inner strain on her face at the prospect of our return to California.

I think of how different my thoughts are now from what they

were during my sojourn at the monastery. In those days, I was still building the walls of my paradigm to withstand the chaos I assumed was beyond them. I simply would not let transient vision and sparks of intuition get out; they wanted to venture beyond the walls into the darkness and I would not allow it.

In those days, I was foolishly holding life's separate parts together. I must have felt that life was predisposed to its own demise. Now, in looking back, I see that it was developing in its own way—not mine.

I am finding that true vision is more often found in disequilibrium than in the mandated balance I was always trying to maintain. Adding to the confusion was my ingrained linear thinking that interpreted reality into separate understandable parts. I am slowly feeling my way beyond the ruins of my paradigm with the thought that my life is more like a free-flowing idea than a mechanism composed of integrated parts.

As soon as I define something or say this part belongs here, it seems to change. I feel like everything I had counted on as factual and grounded by experience is really only in transition on its way to being something else. A single cell grows into a child who matures into a father and that father becomes an old man who, in turn, changes into whatever death is all about. I wonder if it is not all one system, one living bundle of information that unfolds into infinity. Maybe this bundle, this process, is really the only living thing. Perhaps objects that appear in reality are not really alive at all but are only images of a living process in transition.

January 15, 1992

I visit my physician. I've had a few episodes of jagged-edged, blurred vision in the last year, each occurring during times of extreme stress. The doctor thinks the problem is stress-related but wants to be sure. I am scheduled for an MRI, a magnetic resonance imagining, which will show him my brain.

At the MRI facility, I change into a gown and am led down a long hallway by a short, stocky technician. He is a middle-aged man with graying hair and a calm mechanical manner that conveys a sense of boredom with his what he does.

He escorts me into a large room and closes thick metal doors behind us. To my left is a huge machine that all but fills the back wall of the room. In the center of the machine, reaching some ten or twelve feet into its depths, is a long tube, just large enough to accommodate a human body. A narrow, sliding table extends like a sled out on a beam from the mouth of the tube.

I am told to lie down on the table. It was then that a chain of events began to happen. The technician fastened clamps on my temples to hold my head rigidly still. Then, he lowered a mask over my face and locked it in place behind my jaw. The mask had an opening for my nose. Through that opening, I had a narrow corridor of vision.

When he brings the mask down over my face, I immediately think of the day I watched the dark shadow cross Berlyn's face as the funeral director lowered the lid of her coffin for the last time. I begin to sense the presence of death, the same confused unsettled feeling I had the day they sealed Berlyn in her crypt.

Just then, the motor of the table began to buzz and I am lifted up to the opening of the long tube. A vision of Berlyn's crypt flashes before me. With a crank, they had raised the portable table upon which Berlyn's coffin had rested to bring it up to the opening of her crypt.

Suddenly the table begins to move me slowly into the tube. The tip of my nose is less than an inch from the top of the tube and my shoulders scuff along the walls. I close my eyes and swallow hard. My skin begins to crawl as if it is covered with a thousand insects. My heart thunders against my chest.

The deeper I am pushed into the tube, the darker it becomes. The specter of death creeps near to me as it had the day Berlyn was sealed in her tomb. I am deep inside a crypt, hemmed in tight, unable to move. I can barely breathe I am so unnerved. Terror grips every muscle. Something inside me is taking control and wants to escape. It has to get out.

I tell the attendant to stop. He immediately pulls the sled out and unfastens my mask. I sit up. My gown is sticking to my chest with sweat and my hands are trembling. I cannot go through with it.

I return to my office. Never before have I been claustrophobic. A completely new development in my life, it is like having an alien power inside of me about which I know nothing. I am not in control. I am not free. Angry at myself and confused, I am determined to defeat the anxiety, to strangle it. I telephone the MRI facility for another appointment. They have a cancellation for five o'clock the same day.

A few minutes after five o'clock I walk down the already familiar hallway into the chamber with the metal doors. I lie down on the sled. It rises to the gaping mouth of the tube. Death floats suddenly on the air. I breathe it into me in deep halting breaths. I muster all the supporting reason I can to combat the furies that surge within, but I can't. My skin begins to crawl, and my heartbeat quickens.

The technician lowers the mask over my face and locks it in place. I draw a deep breath and close my eyes as I enter the darkness of the tube. Anxiety swells within my chest until I think I will explode from its vibration. Chaos is bursting through the walls of my control and I am drowning in darkness. Death's cold grip caresses me. Again I cannot go through with it.

In a stupor of depression, I stop at a park on my way home and walk among the trees on the outskirts of a baseball field where Berlyn used to play. I am humble beyond anything I can imagine. Whatever cynical toughness I have been able to acquire in life is not nearly as powerful as what I confronted inside the tube. I am humiliated for not being able to withstand the assaults. Like my days as a stuttering child, I feel there is still an alien life form living within me that I do not understand and cannot control.

I look up into golden tendrils of sunlight that stream through the branches of a tall oak. I become still inside. A startling realization dawns on me. Perhaps fear is actually man's struggle against his own gravitation back to chaos. For me, any loss of control will trigger fear.

As a microcosm of what I perceived occurring in human history, I too have projected a human personality onto my fear, creating what seems to be an alien power within me that defends itself against a return to chaos. It also occurs to me that I have hidden from the power as evidenced by my flight from stuttering, among other things.

By understanding my fear for what it is, rather than interpreting it as an alien creature who shares my body, I suddenly feel more in keeping with life's neutrality.

January 16, 1992

Still reeling from my MRI experience, I need to speak with someone who is knowledgeable and yet compassionate. The last thing I need now is a sterile discussion in a clinic. I think of Dr. Perkins who established the Stuttering Center at the University of Southern California. I had been his client some years before.

I recall a time when we were driving to a Hollywood television studio where we were to be the guests on a nationally syndicated talk show to discuss stuttering. For more than a year I had practiced the seven basic skills he had taught me, becoming proficient in using them. He had asked if I would serve as an example of how his treatment works in the interview.

Dr. Perkins knows a great deal about the workings of the mind, but that is not the only reason I trust him with what happened to me inside the MRI. I remember a conversation we shared that day on the way to the studio.

Tall and lean with deep-set hazel eyes, a closely cropped gray beard followed his jaw line, his shirt open at the neck. We drove across town in his antique '59 Mercedes. Having first been an actor before his distinguished academic career, his voice was deep and his pronunciation articulate as we talked.

I am unsure just how we got the subject, but he began telling me the story of his daughter, Alizon. A grade-school student, Alizon was walking to school with her brothers one day when she came to an intersection. The traffic light had turned yellow, but she raced into the street to beat them to the far curb. There was the scream of tires against the pavement. Alizon was dead, her neck broken on impact with a stranger's car.

A light in Dr. Perkins's life had gone out. I saw it in the stoic look on his face that day in the car. Berlyn had been alive then. At the time, I could not fully appreciate his sorrow, but I could certainly see its effects. Now we were linked by shared tragedies. It will be all right to talk with him, I think.

I telephone him. Having recently retired from the university, he invites me to his home. I walk directly into his backyard, with its sweeping view of Los Angeles and find him in work jeans and an untucked flannel shirt, with pruning shears in hand. He is gazing up at a bleeding eucalyptus tree with his hands on his hips when he turns with a look of welcome. "Well, greetings!" he says, with a broad smile.

There is no wall enclosing the yard. A red brick patio blends into a steep forested hillside that spills down into the Los Angeles basin. Beyond is the city, with its distant architectural monuments bathing in the golden haze of a spectacular sunset. He motions to a pair of patio chairs.

The aromas of freshly moistened earth hang in the air, reminding me of memories of the monastery. I begin to talk. "Berlyn's death shattered everything I believed in. It shattered everything that I ever held as a tenet in the universe. Particularly God, my understanding of what all that was. And so what I have tried to do is to trace the beginning of where God came from all the way up to me, so I could find out where I locked into that and what truth there is in it.

"I found out what was plaguing me after her death was fear: fear of evil and fear itself. So I took fear and evil and went back to what I speculated was their inception and brought them forward to myself, so I would not make more of them than what they were. And I figured by understanding the truth of what it is that I could be set free from the bounds of this tragedy.

"When I climbed out of the MRI machine, whatever I believed in seemed a farce. Fear was still operating and in control and that was the most disheartening experience I have ever had: realizing that whatever new reasoning, whatever new beliefs I had, they were not as powerful as the one that was in control—the old nemesis.

"It brought me back to the stuttering example, of why self-hypnosis did not work—because the demon, let's call it, that was inside me, the one that stuttered, was always far more powerful than the self of reason that I was trying to build.

Dr. Perkins asks, "When you stutter, do you feel as if you've lost control of something—the rational you has lost control, probably the conscious you has lost control—of something?"

I answer yes. "It's just like when I was in the MRI machine. All of a sudden my heart started beating rapidly. I didn't ask it to do that. I was covered with sweat, I didn't command that. And I felt anxiety beyond belief, like my chest was going to explode from a multitude of different feelings. It is as if you're a spectator looking at yourself, saying, 'What in the hell is happening to me?' That's stuttering and that was also the MRI thing."

"How did Berlyn's death unleash these furies?"

"When I was driving down to the hospital that night, the first night, when Berlyn was still on that breathing machine, there were things in that dark, dark night. Everything in me surfaced that night, everything I ever feared. Like a schizophrenic—when he watches TV and sees a football game and the camera pans the crowd, it's like the crowd is screaming at him. Everything seemed directed at me, at what I did to cause her death."

"Did you know while you were driving down that she was dead?"

"I knew it. I mean, nobody told me, but I knew it. I told Susan and Morgan that probably we would find that she is dead when we get there and I had kind of already prepared myself for it. Yes, Dr. Perkins, everything that I ever feared in my life has been released by this tragedy. Then the punishment of God, that deity who is vengeful, wrathful, pays you back for everything and you never leave this world without paying and all those kinds of things. When you hear all those things come to the surface you either fight it or you accept it and are condemned forever."

"And that's what you were trying to rebel against, being condemned forever?"

"I think so, yes, because naturally I've done things in my life that are wrong, but I don't understand why such a terrible punishment would come, and come to someone else. And the logical sequence of events didn't fit either. If this forgiving, loving Father figure is omnipresent, he was there, he could have stopped it.

"I didn't understand that and it made me angry that I had been subservient and afraid of this deity and society all of my life and then to have my daughter killed after I had been so subservient—less some foolish mistakes I had tried to fit in. I didn't like the way the thing worked. I didn't like the way the universe worked."

"You frequently speak of humans. You blame humans in general instead of Paul? Why? Are all of us responsible?"

"Society groomed Paul. I don't know, you and I are doing okay. We have a home, food to eat, a wife and a family and all of that, and then there are people like Paul who peer in the window from outside in the cold and they don't have that. It must infuriate the living hell out of them. He was a vengeful kind of a kid, troubled. But he wasn't born that way. What the hell made him that way? He must have had so much hate in him to break out and murder someone that fit the antithesis of himself. When you're talking about blame, I look at Paul as being a stooge, a dupe. But there was something far greater in the scheme of this thing."

"In what way?"

"You have asked why I am able to look at the murder generically, that is, looking at concepts and groups, rather than the actual person. I don't know why that is. Susan even gets mad at me for that, but I just see him as a patsy, a jerk that got swept into this by a power greater than what he was. He wasn't born to do it. He had to learn it. And the system, the way things are, is wrong if it is creating this kind of behavior.

"I also hold God responsible—that whole concept. The believers can't have it both ways. They can't expect miracles, which is intervention in a man's free will, and then say God wouldn't prevent evil because it interferes with your free will. It's either one way or the other.

"And this deity that I've been worshipping all these years, it turns out that He seems like an accomplice to murder to me now. How about those poor Philistines. They were slaughtered by the millions because of God's vengeance on behalf of a selected tribe— the Jews. I can't understand that either. Didn't He make the Philistines, too? The system is wrong—it's all screwed up. And I think that's what produced this guy that killed my daughter. It's this whole background of thinking, from the Old Testament through Greek mythology, all the way through to the present day—it is filled with reasons for Paul to pick up a gun and do what he did righteously."

"So you hold God mainly responsible for Berlyn's murder?"

"No. I hold my concept of God responsible."

"So, it's your fault?"

"In a way."

January 18, 1992

I return to the baseball park where Berlyn used to play and stroll past the oak trees in center field to the edge of a narrow stream that flows around the base of a tall hill. A little girl with long blonde hair and a red baseball cap is playing catch with her father along the left field sidelines. I think back to the days when I threw a ball to Berlyn on that same patch of grass.

I turn away. The MRI experience still weighs on me. Since Berlyn's murder, I have had what I have been told are anxiety attacks; I feel an inner sense of desperation, shortness of breath and an unexplainable need to run until I drop. During these attacks, it seems to me that the self I have fashioned from life is like a cloud through which a lightning bolt passes on its way to its true conductor.

Perhaps life itself is the one and only being that exists of which Berlyn, Susan, Morgan and I are only expressions. Looking outside myself, I can see life's simple neutrality once again. All my days I have obediently judged it, separated it from itself and made myself its center. I suspect now that I have misled myself all the while.

During my periods of anxiousness, a stark feeling emerges that I am essentially alone, like Berlyn. I think about what that feeling means. Perhaps my identity as a human is that feeling of isolation and vulnerability; as a process of life, however, I suspect I am interconnected beyond my ability to comprehend. I think of gravity, magnetic fields, electric fields, even biological fields—fields that tug at me. I have never considered myself as being part of these invisible realities, but I suspect now that I am.

Much of what I used to believe is eroding away—even the soundest of principles. For example, I used to think the speed of light was as fast as anything could move. I suppose I thought this way because I assumed everything had to relate to matter in some way. Now I think of how gravity exerts the same uniform attraction in relation to a mass from one corner of the universe to another—everywhere instantly. A ball bounds down a hillside. Its action conforms to physical influences imposed upon it the instant they occur. Density of the air, angle of the hill, direction and speed of the wind, even the rotation of the earth are all translated into the ball's action in the smallest fractions of time one can measure.

I see a leaf fall from a tree, twisting and turning in a dance with unseen forces. It lights upon the only spot conditions allow—each leaf everywhere.

How are uniformity and conformity instantaneously maintained over great distance? It must be that there is no distance. Space may not really exist. Oneness—nothing is faster.

It also strikes me that a commonality emerging from within these occurrences is intelligence. Can it be that, in addition to oneness, intelligence is faster than the speed of light? I have always associated intelligence with a body part called a brain; my new thinking has me doubting that assumption.

I am beginning to believe consciousness can occur without a brain. I think of how my body's own cells hold genetic messages for their growth and, yet, have no compartmentalized brains. They even have a network of interconnected intelligence, enabling them to duplicate each other's functions. They can also alter their growth and kill me; what happens to me is really up to them and they do not even have brains.

It also appears to me that this intelligence does not share the reasoning of the self I have made, nor does it resemble the personality of the God I had learned about in my childhood. It is a different host altogether. Most everything I have learned has turned out to be wrong. I find now that I have lived in illusion.

Anxiety returns. I recall the brook of my youth. Perhaps my anxious moments are simply waves in life's process, eroding sod from the island I built. If so, I suspect the waves will keep on lapping until I am no more.

January 25, 1992

We had to withdraw Morgan from school today. She has failed every subject; not just the hard ones, every single one. She is devastated by her sister's death. Having been just an average student before, going back to school in the fall following Berlyn's murder in the summer has been simply too much to ask of her.

We find knives under her mattress that she has hidden in case Paul's friends try to kill her. There is something more encompassing gnawing at her, of this we are sure.

It began at her summer basketball camp at Cal State Fullerton a year before Berlyn died. Morgan was entering her dormitory suite after a long day of basketball when she noticed the door to her room was locked. She summoned the student monitor who managed the dormitory during the summer. He unlocked the door and went inside.

Morgan asked him to inspect her room. He did and upon opening the closet door, a man leaped out at him. A fistfight ensued that shocked Morgan to the bone. She ran into the next suite, woke her friend and together they leaped out the back window and scaled a high wire fence, escaping across the common to Berlyn's dormitory room. Morgan raced through the open door into Berlyn's arms. Morgan was in tears and shivering from the shock. Berlyn wrapped her in blankets.

The student monitor happened to be a member of the university's wrestling team and he managed to subdue the intruder and turn him over to the police. I heard from camp officials the next day that the man who had been hiding in Morgan's closet was a wanted criminal.

A few weeks after Berlyn's murder, Morgan had called me into her room. She was lying in bed, worry all over her face. "There's something after us. It's like I told you. I just know it. First that awful man in my room and now Berlyn. It's after us. Oh, Daddy, I'm so scared."

I sat on the edge of the bed and held her as she cried. Her hand felt cold as it quivered against the back of my neck. "What am I going to do? What am I going to do? It's after us, Dad."

She was certain that the devil, planted in her budding paradigm by religious teachers, was on the loose and now it was after our family. I tried to console her, but behind my words, I carried the same fears from my own childhood.

Paul and other violent people like him do not realize how they contribute to a frightening pattern, especially for the children they indirectly abuse. They become the programmers who control lives long after their terrible deeds.

When Paul fired his gun, he hit Morgan, too.

Susan has resigned from her job to become Morgan's home-school teacher. Morgan has moved into Berlyn's room. Earlier today, they made a game of redecorating Morgan's old bedroom into a classroom. They worked excitedly, but behind the exuberant veneer, Susan is deeply worried about Morgan, who I suspect, is as sad as she is embarrassed to be disconnected from the educational system and her friends.

Several days ago, Morgan nestled onto my lap and together we watched the stars for a while. "Dad," she said, "if only Berlyn would come and hold me just one more time, it would be easier for me. Know what I mean?"

She burrowed her forehead into the nape of my neck. It was all unraveling and she could not hold it back. Life was nearly out of control. The forces that had slammed into her were far too powerful for a young girl to handle. "Oh, Daddy, I miss her so much," she cried.

This evening while I sit beneath the stars, she comes outside and sits on the lawn next to my chair. "Berlyn, came to me last night like I had hoped she would, Dad."

"She did?"

"She came to me in a dream. She stood just inside the doorway of her room, well—my room now. She said, 'You asked me to come and hold you.'

"Oh, Dad, it was Berlyn. I know it was her. I got out of bed and hugged her. She even let me touch the wart on her shoulder so I would know it was true. I kissed her, Dad, and then, well, she went away."

I respond with all the tenderness I can muster. "I'm glad she came to you, sweetheart. She loved you so much."

Later that night after Morgan is asleep, Susan tells me that, when she went to wake Morgan up this morning, she had found her asleep on the floor by the door to her room exactly where she said Berlyn had hugged her. Involuntarily my eyes filled.

January 27, 1992

At the end of our previous meeting, Dr. Perkins asked if I would be willing to come back to talk about how my feelings resulting from Berlyn's murder connect to stuttering. I started, "In the aftermath of stuttering is terrible loneliness, then I would leave an appointment and it was dark and I would walk outside and have camaraderie with God because I was the suffering, I was the meek, I was the humbled, I was the chastised."

"So your stuttering brought you down? You saw stuttering as punishment because it's embarrassing, yet after you've been chastised you feel in tune with your deity. That must be very rewarding."

"Yes, it is."

"So that means stuttering has a big payoff to counterbalance the embarrassment."

"Yes."

"This is interesting because one of the few consistent physiological findings about stuttering is that it is a powerful mechanism for reducing stress. This has never made sense to me, but we tested two dozen people who stutter and all of them had a much greater reduction in stress after stuttering than after anything else that reduces stress. You've just given me a clue as to why this may happen."

"So now I was on a plane with the martyrs or the saints. I could have a creative interaction with this deity that, in those moments, had sympathy for me, liked me. But then it was always perplexing. If I was that endearing to this entity when I was in the lowest depths of my life, why in the hell would it not rescue me—the last straw being Berlyn's death?"

Dr. Perkins interrupted. "The situations in which your personal power is in jeopardy is where the stuttering arises?"

"Yes. I came to a stark realization of that when having the MRI. I was locked in it and the thing was put over me, just like the lid being closed on a casket, I was being put into a crypt. There was a feeling of being without any control. I asked the guy if he would please do me the favor of showing me how to unhook the hood so if an earthquake—I would be able to get out of there, I could unhook it, and he said I could not do that. And that is when he locked it. I couldn't get my head out of this machine if I had to unless he came down from the booth and did it. I was without the power to save myself.

"I can remember being in classrooms as a kid and worrying about stuttering. Teachers would often go around the room in order asking students to read orally—one after the other. I would look up at the clock every few minutes trying to figure if class time would run out before it would be my turn. Most times, I was trapped with no way out.

"If there were one common denominator between the two experiences, it was a lack of escape."

"So the fear, then, was the helplessness—the powerlessness came from having your escape route cut off," said Dr. Perkins. "When you had to say your name you would have no escape. How far back does all of this explanation go?"

"I have always felt a sense of evil that overwhelms me when I stutter. But as much as it bothered me, I could never really make sense of it. Berlyn's murder opened the floodgates. I had no idea how full I was of ideas about God, religion, the Bible, mythology. I knew I was interested in these things, but I never knew how much until she was killed. I hadn't a clue how profound my assumption was that God was benevolent, protective, loving—and vengeful. I can't tell you how punished I feel. My guess is that everyone has a lot of deep assumptions floating around in them that they don't even suspect they have until some tragedy awakens them."

Dr. Perkins replies, "Split-brain research has demonstrated that when the two halves of the brain are disconnected, they can contain very different answers to the same question. What you're conscious of knowing is typically in the left hemisphere that controls speech. Where the left hemisphere is primarily concerned with logic and rational thinking, the other hemisphere is more involved in feelings and emotions. So when you answer a question, your answer reflects only what the language hemisphere knows, which is not necessarily the correct answer. What research shows is that a fundamental function of this hemisphere is to make sense of whatever information it has, which would seem to you to be correct, even though it may not be. In your case, the fear probably came from circumstances in infancy—so early you didn't have language to fathom or explain what was happening to you. Later, when you had to explain stuttering to yourself, and now when you have to explain Berlyn's murder, you had no choice but to use whatever information was available to the language hemisphere, which is all that you know you know."

February 1, 1992

Barry, an old, old friend of mine, calls and wants to get together. He had been a pallbearer at Berlyn's funeral. (Funeral. Even associating the word with Berlyn still has me shaking my head in disbelief.) Since her death, Barry had frequently been out of town on business and, though we had met for lunch on occasion, we had little opportunity to really talk.

Broad-shouldered and strongly built, Barry wears conservative gray suits that are barely distinguishable one from the other. With his wire-rimmed glasses, he looks like a figure you would find staring back at you from a 1930s photograph. Though he struggles with himself to be more daring in his choice of cars and clothes, he always winds up still being Barry—honest and sincere. I guess that's why my family and I like him so much.

Another characteristic about Barry that I find endearing is when he grins he reminds me of Jay. They share the same broad smile. When Barry played basketball at the park with Berlyn and me he would have to work against his innate awkwardness, much like Jay. In the end, he had to will himself to play games.

After he visits for a while with Morgan and Susan, we drive high up into the Angeles Forest. I park the car between two pines and together we start walking to wherever the dirt fire road will take us. We have no destination. Our need is to be above the city in the serene quiet where we can talk.

The air is cool in the shadows of the pines but the rays of the afternoon sun are warm. We leave our jackets in the car, our sweatshirts are enough to keep us comfortable. The mountain air smells refreshingly sweet as opposed to the smog of Los Angeles. Barry picks a tall grass stem from the roadside and holds it in his lips.

"What has been happening with you since the trial?" he asks, a look of concern on his face. "You've been kind of isolated. Frankly, I've been a little worried."

After all the struggles and conflicts I've faced on my journey, his question staggers me for a moment. There is too much to tell. For the first time, I realize just how private and even secret my journey to the new universe and Berlyn has been. A new fascination has begun to sweep me along my solitary road, though. It has to do with the lost heritage Berlyn and I shared.

"Lately, I've been giving a lot of my time to the study of genetics."

"Genetics?" he retorts. "Why genetics?"

"Everything about Berlyn and, for that matter, the personality of life itself, were represented in her genetic chemistry. There was so much more to her than what I noticed while she was with me. Even though she's gone, I still want to know all I can about her."

He looks out questioningly over the deep forested valley. Ahead, the road wraps around the mountain on an incline to the valley floor. "You know, I never thought about genetics as a way of understanding someone, know what I mean? I had always associated genetics with physical traits and the root cause of disease. I guess that's because I was never pressed into looking at it in the way you have. Tell me."

"Well, I'm finding out that genetic material is really the physical representation of who we are. You know, like barnacles that arrange themselves around a wooden piling in the sea, it takes on the form of what we are, defining us in a way. Know what I mean?"

"Could it be, then, that genetic material expresses what we call the soul?" he asked.

"Could be, I guess, if that's where you're coming from." Barry is one of those good people, I reconfirm to myself, with the rare ability to lose himself in the needs of others. I sense he has come here for me, to let me talk and explain things to myself. He will simply be a catalyst by listening. That is Barry's way. A less enlightened person would try to offer explanations and solutions, but not Barry. He will help me find my own. I am grateful to have a friend like him.

"As I understand it," I went on, "genetic material is nothing more than information. Primal elements that had drawn together in that very special sequence to create Berlyn were like volumes of information about her. Of course, they also contain the story of our human family, and perhaps even the gods who created us, if indeed they did. I am sure she knew little of what she was during her brief time in matter. I believe it is this meaning that is represented by our genetic sequence that is eternal. In other words, the meaning that gave rise to us survives us."

"What do you think was Berlyn's meaning?" he asks.

"I believe she was simply information about life. It occurs to me that one day our genetic sequence will prove a far better introduction of us than even a personal meeting."

I shove my hands into the pockets of my jeans. "You know, I believe that whenever elements in chaos are reconfigured in her special sequence, Berlyn will again be the result. It's like when the sums of two and two are brought together, four will automatically appear.

"Maybe the time that would duplicate her is traveling away from me now." I thought of Jupiter's lonely voyage away from Mars and Venus that I had witnessed each night from my backyard. "But, perhaps the universe is elliptical and, if it is, someday her time will arch back around. I have the hope that at the end of all other mathematical possibilities the essence of Berlyn will have circled life's encasement to reconfigure again. Perhaps that is what all the great ones meant when they said they would return."

Barry shakes his head, his eyes shut, then looks over at me with a grin. "That's deep stuff. You've really been on a journey, haven't you."

February 10, 1992

It is early evening. I am driving in the car with Susan in the passenger seat beside me. I am curious about how her feelings are evolving toward Paul, wanting to test them against my own.

"You know my feelings about Paul," I open. "What are yours now that some time has passed?"

"I feel the second he pulled the trigger, he was dead. There's no future for him. He blew his own life away, too. I hate what he did. I will always hate what he did. I don't wish him harm, but it wouldn't bother me if he never had a happy day the rest of his life.

She paused. "I remember when we were at the high school basketball game the other evening. Paul's mother walked into the gym with her two sons. I felt a sense of rage. I remember her comment to the media."

"What comment?" I ask.

"Oh, when she said 'My son is a good boy.' First of all, he's not a boy; he's a man. Second, he's not good; he's a murderer.

"I guess I try not to think too much about him. It's too horrible. I've buried him. To me, people like him are leeches. After he shot Berlyn, everyone else had to clean up his mess—paramedics, doctors, the police, you and I. We had to pay all the expenses he caused and bear the awful burdens he left us with. He didn't have to pay for a thing. It was all done for him—his attorney, the courts, everything. His only inconvenience is he can't go out to play. We're even paying for him now and we'll continue to pay.

"Now, for peace of mind, we're having to send Morgan to a different high school—one that is out of town. She can't go to school with her friends any more; Paul decided that for her when he pulled the trigger. That's what people like that do to you. It's not fair. We never infringed upon Paul's family, but because of their encroachment on ours, we have to do all the changing. They simply entrench themselves and force us to make the decisions. They don't have to be inconvenienced, we do, and we're the victims. We have to bear the expense and daily hardships in helping Morgan start over. If we don't like it, that's tough. We have to turn our lives upside down, but they won't. It's not fair, but there it is. Now I have all this anger. I didn't put it there. I didn't choose to carry it with me, but there it is anyway."

February 15, 1992

I am sitting at another long mahogany table in a dark paneled boardroom. The plush black leather swivel chair is soft and comfortable. I survey the twenty or so people that occupy places around the table. They are average-looking, nothing sets them apart. It is the boardroom of the Pasadena Police Headquarters and I am attending a meeting of parents whose children have been murdered.

My very first reaction is a familiar one, a wave of disbelief for having a reason to be there in the first place. It is the same feeling I experienced during Paul's trial. Why has my life with Berlyn brought me here among these tragic people I ask myself. I still cannot accept the full impact of what has happened.

I keep glancing around me at the faces of the people who have lived unimaginable horror, searching for a telltale sign, a minute trace of difference that I can recognize, but there is none. They are, essentially, the neighbors next door. And so I slip silently into one of the most emotionally draining experiences I have ever known.

The leader of the meeting is a tall, slender, elderly man. He sports a white receding crew cut and a somewhat weathered face, befitting a man who once earned his living outdoors as a tradesman. He explains that the purpose of the gathering is for each person to share the story of his or her child's murder. It is voluntary. I assume the hoped-for outcome is that each of us discovers that in our uniquely horrible circumstances we are not alone.

An attractive blonde woman in her early forties looks hard at me from the far end of the table. "When I read about your daughter and saw the television accounts, it all came back to me," she says and draws a handkerchief up to catch the tear in eye. As if orchestrated by a conductor, the twenty or so men and women around the table turn their gazes upon me.

In a shaky voice choked with pain, she recounts how her teenaged daughter and a girl friend had been partying one day with some boys, three I believe she said, in their pool house. She turns her eyes directly on me as she struggles to retell her nightmare.

An argument ensued later that evening with at least two of the boys. Thought to be under the influence of drugs, the two boys had stormed from the party and driven off through the upscale neighborhood. Apparently, they first went home where they collected a couple of shotguns and then returned to the pool party.

Like Berlyn, the woman's daughter had already gone to sleep on the couch by the time the boys returned. For reasons unknown, one of the boys put the barrel of the shotgun to the back of her daughter's head and calmly pulled the trigger, blowing the back of her skull to pieces. Remorselessly, they turned to the other girl and shot her to death as well.

By the end of the story, the woman is holding her face in her hands, sobbing uncontrollably. Tears drip from between her knuckles. I want to tell her something, anything that will ease her pain, but know there is little I can do for her besides listen.

Expectant stares turn to the next woman, who, she relates has a missionary background. She and her husband have served one of the foreign missions of their church for many years. She is in her late forties, neatly dressed, with dark-rimmed glasses that contrast starkly with her pale complexion. A warm smile shines through her solemn expression.

It has been a few years since her tragedy, so she is able to tell her sad tale without obvious distress. Her voice is purposeful, as if calculatedly normal. Her story progresses robotically from word to word as if she has told it many times before.

Her daughter, a young married woman, had visited a nearby mall one evening near closing time when two men abducted her off the escalator. They took her to a remote area near the Rose Bowl, where they repeatedly assaulted her. Minutes before the police arrived on the scene, they shot her in the back of the head. "If only the police had been a minute earlier," she ends, with a sigh of resignation.

I wonder how this mother with her missionary background has struggled with the meaning of her daughter's murder. She appears to me to be confidently back in the fold, deep within the safe confines of her paradigm.

Before they go on to the next person, I ask her what the murder has done to her beliefs, hoping to find that she has ventured out into the frontier as I have. I need an exchange with someone like her, someone who had made a commitment to a belief that has not withstood reality.

She replies that she and her husband spent many hours together trying to fathom the experience, but in the end, they simply surrendered to the God of the Garden of Eden and remained within the world they had created for themselves.

I am disappointed. I want so much to meet someone who is risking a pilgrimage from what they were. A good woman, she is resolutely ascending to the highest levels of her religious paradigm by giving up understanding for faith.

We go around the room, hearing the stories, and then the opportunity to speak comes to the elderly leader. He reports that he was the grandfather of a high school girl who, while waiting for the morning school bus, was abducted by two men. Her mother, the leader's daughter, had looked out the window on hearing the school bus horn and noticed her daughter's musical instrument and books on the ground, but no sign of her youngster.

The abductors had taken the girl to a deserted building where they repeatedly raped her and then made several clumsy attempts to kill her. First they tried to strangle her with a piece of fabric by wrapping it around her neck and pulling on it, but she refused to die. They finally ended up stabbing her to death.

I cringe inside from the description and I feel my heart literally ache for that girl. In my mind's eye, I am standing silently inside a dimly lit, dust-covered barn. Yellow rays of morning sunlight streak onto the dirt floor through the spaces between warped gray boards along the wall. Before me are two shirtless killers, their muscles straining against a rag wrapped around an angelic teenage girl's neck. They grunt and sweat through their work of strangling the life from her. The young girl's eyes bulge and her mouth gapes open as she desperately gasps for the air that would keep her alive a few more minutes. I force myself to see something different.

After about an hour of the most tragic tales I have ever heard, suddenly, all eyes turned to me. I swallow hard and began to recount the details of my living nightmare. As I speak I am simultaneously fending off the onslaught of emotions that are rushing against me, but my defenses are so low that I am overcome.

Then, I find myself caught in that awful dilemma of having to relate my tale through painfully constricted throat muscles while wrestling against overpowering emotions. Through it all, I wonder why I am damming up my own need to cry. I suppose it is another foolish part of the person I had made, one that I no longer understand.

After finishing my story, I confess my fear that, by some metaphysically way, I might have caused Berlyn's death. I feel exposed after opening my darkest worry to strangers, but I want to draw someone out who can give me a measure of nurturing advice.

It would be like medicine on an open festering wound. I am glad I have taken the risk.

A broad-shouldered man in a charcoal suit sits directly across from me. His teenaged son had been stabbed in the heart and killed during a robbery. I see his bushy dark eyebrows come together in a scowl, he aims a thick finger between my eyes as he says sternly, "The only person who killed your daughter is the man who shot her." I feel a weight lift from me.

February 25, 1992

I am having lunch with Barry in Westwood's Moustache Cafe, a French restaurant near UCLA.

As we finish our business, I watch Barry's face grow somber. "I really value the conversation we had in the mountains the other day," he says, casually buttering a roll. "You've had me thinking ever since. Let me ask you something—that is, if you don't mind talking more about it." He paused.

"I don't mind. Go ahead."

"Well, I guess the question I was left with is have you found the reason you were looking for? You know, about why Berlyn died."

"Not really. For me, there's always the lingering specter of metaphysical intervention hovering over her murder. You know, those invisible causes like luck, miracles and, I guess, fate.

"I remember you told me once that you thought we had our origins in chaos. Maybe there are no reasons for what happens to us. Maybe it's a part of our heritage in chaos that came out with us, like a virus. Know what I mean?"

"Could well be."

He takes a sip of iced tea, sets down his glass and sits back against his chair, grinning at me from behind his glasses. It is Jay's grin. His look would seem out of place, given the nature of our conversation, but that is Barry's mask—a perpetual grin.

For a moment, my thoughts turn to my childhood home and those uncomplicated summer days in the sacred woods. I turn to face a warm sunbeam that streaks through the European-style window across the room, but thoughts of a cruel spiritual influence reenter my mind. The possibility of such a force has been an enigma to me since Berlyn's murder.

"Well, the intervening force about which I was so concerned was, in all truthfulness, morality and had to do with the daughter I chose to give away. Does moral action produce predictable consequences? That was, for me, the great question that Berlyn's murder has evoked. I was continually suffering from the moral guilt of having abandoned my firstborn among other things I had done in my life, that all together might have left Berlyn vulnerable somehow. I can't explain it exactly, but it is how I felt. It may sound bizarre to you, but when I first began to personalize Berlyn's murder, moral connections began to arise everywhere."

"That's bunk," he retorts. "I remember how you were torturing yourself with those thoughts right after the funeral. I still believe it doesn't happen that way. Life isn't set up like that."

"In any case," I continue, "I've since taken a hard look at where I was coming from at the time Berlyn was killed. Since I was a kid, I always believed there was a direct relationship between moral actions and the consequence of those actions. What I mean is, I believed that life always reflected back to me what I had done, or, at least, that was my interpretation of events. You know, if I was good, good things seemed to happen to me and if I was bad, well, it seemed bad things would happen."

"Yeah, I can relate to that."

"The 'paybacks,' if you will, were as reliable to me as mathematics. However, the form these reflections would take was always an unpredictable mystery. It always kept me kind of on guard. Do you know what I mean?"

"Yes, I do," he says in a tone that suggests he carries the suspicions too.

"I could really never verify my assumptions analytically because results were so subjective. Different observers could never achieve the same results. Yet, when the consequences of moral actions arrived, they appeared unmistakably related to what I had assumed precipitated them. I also suspect that I am not alone in thinking this way."

"I guess a lot of us look at life that way."

"I also find that moral causes, which I once believed to be universal mandates from God, differ widely from one culture to another. Another complication is that they are often attributed consequences that have no consistent pattern. Lightning strikes the good and the bad; the innocent are murdered along with the guilty, and so on.

"From my new perspective, I have come to find that life may be neutral and not based upon human- or God-inspired judgment at all. Morality's consequences, I now feel, are limited to the society for which they were created. Because we are only mortal, I also believe that our sins are no more infinite or powerful than we are."

"Congratulations!" he exclaims, feigning applause, causing some stuffy executives at nearby tables to glance our way.

Just then, a wave of grief washes over me. I busy myself eating. Why do I have to try to understand it all? Why did she have to die? Sometimes, I just want everything to be simple as it used to be. I do not want to have to find a new universe. I want the old one with Berlyn. The furies are rising within my chest again. Even though Barry is just across the table, I am again alone.

February 28, 1992

I think of Paul and his imprisonment and I wonder what bizarre encounters have already become commonplace for him.

Again, it turns my thoughts to my own experiences in the jail infirmary during my year tenure there.

There was a time when a short Puerto Rican man in his late thirties appeared in our sick-call line. He wore blue denims and had been serving a short sentence for domestic violence. "I'm feeling nervous," he said to the doctor who grinned around the cigar in his mouth. The inmate ran his thick fingers through his curly black hair and looked down. "I get out today and I don't know what I'm gonna do."

"You get out today and you're nervous about that?!" the doctor exclaimed, jokingly. "Well, there's a hell of a lot of guys in here who would love to have your problem." He took the cigar from his mouth and joined in the laughter with the other inmates who were in line. The Puerto Rican forced a grin, but it quickly fell away. "Okay, here," the doctor said in a kind voice and gave the man a couple of pills.

Two days later, the inmate was escorted to the infirmary by a pair of guards. He was in khakis this time and there was blood on his shoes. I had heard that the day he was released from the jail, he went to the home of his estranged wife, where he murdered her and their three children with a machete. Rumor in the jail had it that he had chopped off their heads.

He had been assigned to the infirmary, which was routine for the most disturbed criminals. He was lying on a bed just outside my door, reading comic books. I was sitting at my desk filling out his paperwork when I looked up and found him staring in at me through the barred door. "Hey, come here, please," he said as he motioned to me. I walked over to him. "He began to speak in a whisper. "Hey man, why am I here? What did I do?"

"You don't know?" I questioned.

"No. They brought me in here, but they won't tell me why."

Evidently, he had blocked the murders from his mind. He

reminded me of a young inmate I had in the infirmary in August of that year. He had beaten his mother to death with a hammer. About 20 years old, he was a tall boy with a pale, white complexion. I had assigned him the same bed as I had the Puerto Rican. Now that I think of it, I believe he spent his first day reading the same comic books.

The lieutenant had come to check on the condition of the new inmate and stopped in my office to ask me about him. The officer's tan and green uniform was starched smooth, and there was that familiar bundle of keys hanging from his black belt. The biggest one on his ring was a black key that fit the solitary section. It hung down farther than the rest—like a warning. He was in his late thirties, with receding hair slicked down and combed back straight. To me, he always wore what appeared to be a sadistic smirk. He was one of the rare guards who actually loved his job. "How's our new guy out there?"

"I don't know. He lies there reading comic books, like he's not aware of what he's done," I answered.

"He's not aware of it," the lieutenant grinned. "Give him three days, then it'll dawn on him." He laughed. "Then he'll howl good."

The lieutenant had called it right. Three days later, at night, the young man was on all fours atop his bed, howling out the window like a wolf at the moon. It was bone-chilling to hear. The lieutenant stopped by, peered in and chuckled at him.

February 29, 1992

I finish the last game in a long season of coaching. It marks the end of my fifth year as a volunteer coach for the girls' basketball team. I began with Berlyn and then brought Morgan into the program when she was only eight years old. During that time, I have found nothing more humbling than chastising a little girl for her play only to have her look up at me with wide eyes and a sweaty face to say, "Okay, coach, thanks."

The girls and their parents have all gone home. The gymnasium is empty. I lock the outside doors and turn off the rows of lights that hang from ceiling rafters. The gym suddenly darkens— only a light in the hall on the second level and the red exit signs over the doors glow. The darkness reminds me of the woods behind my childhood home.

The empty gym has contained so much emotion within its tall concrete walls, giving the place a personality of its own. I put my duffle bag down and sit on the first row of bleachers.

Through the darkness I look down the court at the shadowy form of the far basket and recall a post-season summer tournament in which I had coached Berlyn in this same gym. She was a junior in high school at the time. The score was 51—50 and we were behind with only six seconds left. I called for a time-out and brought the girls together in a huddle.

"Okay," I told them, "we've only six seconds. Here's what to do. Inbound the ball to Berlyn and let her do what she can." I had a feeling she would somehow come through. She was a champion and that quality would rise to meet the challenge. It was our best bet given the time that was left.

"That's it?" one girl asked with a scowl.

"That's it," I responded flatly.

The referee handed the ball to our girl on the sideline. Berlyn raced into the clear to receive her pass with two opposing players close behind. She caught the ball and dribbled up the court at breakneck speed, weaving through the opposition as if they were posts nailed to the floor.

One of the girls guarding her was fast and very agile. She kept pace with Berlyn, forcing her away from the basket. Time was running out. Berlyn jumped way up from a running stride and flicked the ball with her wrist. The buzzer blared over the screams of the crowd as the ball arched down. An ever-lasting second finally passed and the ball exploded through the net. I remembered my thought at that exact moment: Champions just do it.

When the girls mobbed her on the floor, Berlyn looked over at me. It was just a glance, but it said a lot. Her eyes told me she had given me something uniquely hers. Neither one of us knew what it was, but we both marveled at it. There was also a glint of gratitude in her eyes for my recognition of who she was and for having trusted my sense about her.

Then, darkness enfolds me and I am reminded of her death. The wrenching grief comes in waves and often without warning.

I lean back against the bleachers and fold my arms on my chest. A song on the radio or a stroll in the sunset down a wooded path where Berlyn and I once walked can set me off. Worse still are the mysterious waves of anxiety that simply attack me with no apparent reason.

It seems to me that when emotions from the past are preferred over those of the present, grief results. With Berlyn's death, the anchor point for a great deal of my love is suddenly missing. As a result, my love seems to spoil, turning into the terrible pain I experience as grief.

I walk out onto the floor and stand beneath the backboard, looking up at the hoop. Soft yellow light cascades down between concrete pillars, like a dim spotlight from a distant world. I glance over at the bench on the other side of the court where Berlyn often sat. Her salt is probably still ingrained in the wood, I think to myself.

March 6, 1992

It is the early morning hours before dawn. I am in a deep sleep. Suddenly, I am jolted awake by a sharp, deafening explosion and a flash of light. I sit up gasping for breath and quickly look around the room. I can feel my heart pounding against my chest. What happened? That's odd, I think, when I see Susan still asleep beside me. Didn't she hear it? I am ready to race upstairs for Morgan when the realization of what has happened hits me. I had heard the gunshot. I grip the blankets to keep my hands from shaking and sit on the edge of the bed, stunned, staring into the darkness.

The more I contemplate what has just happened, the calmer I become, as if a soothing mist begins to fall upon me. I have just experienced a reenactment of the last millisecond of Berlyn's life. As horrifying an illusion as it is, I am thankful to have shared what I imagine to be possibly the last sound she heard and the last flash of light she saw before the end.

March 10, 1992 – Enroute to China

Some months ago I organized an event in support of the Volunteers of America's China Project. It is a program designed to serve American volunteers who wish to offer their expertise to people and businesses in developing nations as ambassadors of good will. To help us launch the initial wave of volunteer experts, Ross Perot agreed to receive the organization's first Marco Polo Award. Proceeds from patrons of the award are used to send our volunteer experts to China.

I am going to China to represent the Volunteers of America of Los Angeles in signing agreements with the government there and to interview industry leaders seeking American experts. Susan and Morgan are with me. I know the experience will be as welcome an adventure for them as it will be timely. So long as Morgan is in home-school, she will not fall behind.

We land in Beijing, where we are met by an official delegation representing the City of Tianjin's Municipal People's Government, our hosts for the first week of our visit. Following one day to rest, we tour the Forbidden City and, the next day, China's Great Wall. Then we set off for Tianjin. I am happy to be here. Berlyn played on a southern California all-star basketball team that toured China just after her junior year. It had been the landmark of her basketball career until she received her scholarship.

Once in Tianjin, I begin a demanding schedule of factory tours, visits to farming cooperatives and day and evening banquets with government officials. Susan and Morgan join me for much of it. For our stay we are assigned a vehicle, complete with driver, a translator and an official delegation. When Susan and Morgan would rather tour or shop while I work, a car, driver and translator are made available for them as well. The hospitality of the Chinese leaves nothing wanting.

At one point, I visit Tianjin University of Economics and Finance. The Vice Mayor of the city, knowing how involved I am in girls' basketball, arranges for Morgan to have the distinct privilege of playing in a special intersquad game of the university's women's basketball team.

I sit between Susan and the university's president at a long courtside dais in what was a spectacular modern gymnasium. Our delegation fills the remaining places on either side. I am deeply grateful for the experience, as it gives Morgan the chance to follow in Berlyn's pioneering footsteps.

It is our last evening in Tianjin. A private party is held in our honor at the home of a member of our delegation. Following dinner, we are treated to dance music. Just then, the room fills with an instrumental version of *Auld Lang Syne*. The song always creates a reflective somber mood in me under the best of conditions, on New Year's Eve, but I had not heard it since Berlyn's death. I stand in a corner of the room with my eyes closed, immersed in the music, as Susan and Morgan dance merrily with our hosts on the crowded floor.

Then, the lyrics pour into my mind. *"Should old acquaintance be forgot . . . and never brought to mind. Should old acquaintance be forgot and days of auld lang syne."*

March 17, 1992

Yesterday we flew to Shanghai, where I had a private meeting with the government leader overseeing our visit. I asked to visit a Buddhist temple and to have the opportunity to speak with a monk. I told him about Berlyn. He closed his eyes and nodded. Early in the morning, I am whisked away to a renowned Buddhist temple on the outskirts of Shanghai. There, I am met by Reverend Sek Miao Ling, director of the temple, the abbot of the monastery.

He is tall, in his late thirties, with a youthful smiling face and a shaved head. He wears a tan pastel robe over what appears to be a gray sweatshirt. Round, wire-rimmed glasses are the only signs of the twentieth century. My translator, Yunjie, who has adopted the name Jenny, is a petite, attractive Chinese woman in her early twenties. Her shoulder-length ebony hair and matching sweater contrast starkly with her smooth porcelain complexion. Her voice is soft and her English articulate.

I follow her through pagoda-like buildings packed with worshippers and filled with clouds of incense. Gigantic jade and gold-plated Buddhas tower over us. Other god-like statues, some with fierce, scowling expressions, others with placid somber ones, gaze down at us. Their golden eyes seem to follow me.

My tour ends at a small sitting room on the second level of one of the temple buildings. The entire floor outside the room is a vegetarian restaurant open to the public, the means by which the monastery supports itself. We sit at a table with Jenny at my side and

Reverend Sek across the table. Tea is brought in by an oblate. The morning is damp and cold. I hold the cup in my hands relishing the warmth. The reverend waits patiently.

After thanking him for his time, I take a deep breath and tell him the story of Berlyn's murder. The grin never leaves his face. He simply nods at Jenny's explanation and glances over at me as he holds a string of prayer beads between his folded hands. I finished, then got to the point.

"For a long time after Berlyn's murder, I felt that because of what I perceived to be transgressions against the Judeo/Christian God of my heritage, I had contributed to the cause of my daughter's death. By the light you have been given, could that have been true?"

Jenny's delicate voice fell soothingly on me as she translated Reverend Sek's reply. "No, her death did not come from you. There are requirements for a human being to live. For example, one first has to have a spirit and then a man and woman must be joined together. There are many more. There were no requirements for your daughter beyond the time of her death."

His answer is inexplicable to me. I am instantly disappointed, but push the reaction aside to ask: "Where is she now?"

"She has already been reborn. She is living again as someone else."

I cannot grasp his answer. His smile turns to a frown. "Why do you seek to possess her? She is no longer your daughter."

Inwardly cringing, I let his answer pass through me without a twinge of reaction on the outside and manage to ask yet another question. Somehow I will fit the pieces of all this together later. "The God I grew up with has a human-like personality with traits of love, hatred, joy and sorrow. Does such a being fit with your understanding of what rules our universe?"

"No," Jenny said, echoing his answer. "Such a being comes

from your imagination." He hit squarely upon the conclusion I had come to. Suddenly, I am amidst familiar surroundings again. I revel at the thought that I had discovered for myself what an ancient pilgrim found centuries ago. My kinship with humanity starts to rekindle.

"Like a projection from myself onto life?"

"Yes. Exactly," Jenny replies as she turns to face me. "Buddhism," she continues, "tells you about the rules—what to expect from life. In Christianity, God is in control. To the Buddhist, control lies with the individual. You are your own god. What you call God is simply 'the rules.'"

"By rules, you mean life? Life is what I had known as God. Am I right?"

"Yes. There is no human-like father-god; there is only life and Buddhism tells you what to expect from it. For example, it tells you that there is origination, then there is existence for a period of time, followed by change and, finally, everything disappears. Birth, age, disease and death. Nothing can escape these four phases of life."

We both sip at our cups of tea. I study him over the rim of my cup. He grins. I nod to myself. He is on his pilgrimage and I am on mine. We are brothers in a way, though, for him, there is no heaven or hell and no heavenly father to appease. We have viewed life from different paradigms.

April 10, 1992

On my way to work I drive past Paul's old apartment by the freeway. More jail memories involuntarily come to my mind as I imagine experiences awaiting him. One image I had from my past was of an elderly inmate from Poland. He was a short, gaunt-looking man with thin reddish hair and thick glasses. The index fingers on both his hands were yellow-brown from holding smoldering cigarettes. I sat by his bed one day when, in broken English, he told me how he had escaped from a concentration camp in Poland during World War II.

One night close to the end of the war a German guard was patrolling a destroyed section of fence near where the inmate was hiding in the shadows by the side of a building. There was corrugated metal on the ground between the guard and him that would act as an alarm if a prisoner trampled over it while trying to escape. "I had to take the chance," he said. "It was either rush the guard and silence him or die in that place. So I went for him with a metal tool in my hand and before he could use his rifle, I smashed in his skull."

He went on to tell me that he made his way through Poland by riding under a railroad car. "In those days," he explained, "the entire axle would spin. Look, I have these deep scars from where it was grinding against my back." He turned over and showed me rough keloid scars. He eventually reached Spain, and freedom.

Now he was in jail awaiting trial for killing his landlady. He had been arguing with her over something having to do with his apartment. She had threatened to call the police. "I grew up very fearful of police," he explained to me. "So, when she threatened to bring them, I struck her and she died. I was so afraid of being discovered by the authorities that I chopped her into small pieces and put them to the furnace."

April 19, 1992

It is late by the time I arrive home from work. As I put my key in the door, Susan opens it and smiles. I give her a kiss. Being there at the door with a smile is a signal that she is feeling better. It seems like such a small thing to notice, but after living with someone for a quarter century, signs of affection can take the simplest of forms.

I am beginning to recognize our bond as being made from the stuff of life rather than intellect or arrangement. We are both alone and together. It is all so different now. Like so many others before us who have had to pick up the pieces of their lives, we are no different.

April 20, 1992

I am awakened by a nightmare, which brings back memories of some of the earlier dreams I experienced soon after Berlyn's murder.

The first, only a few nights after her death, found me standing at the stern of a sleek, white cabin cruiser. In the background, I saw the Brooklyn Bridge. Suddenly, the huge, black iron bow of a barge roars in the fog. The barge is bearing down on me. I climb quickly below deck into a cramped galley where Susan is preparing vegetables. "Hurry," I urge in a voice that seems too calm for the situation. "Hurry, there's a . . ." Just then, the giant hulk rams through the stern of our boat and with the grating din of buckling metal, vaults up onto the deck above my head. Over my shoulder I see the bulkheads crack and watch as we are pressed down into the swirling water.

Good dreams have visited me as well. Like Morgan, I want Berlyn to acknowledge me. I needed her to kiss me just once more. That kiss has to last me the rest of my life.

Just a few days after making that wish, I am in a dream sitting on a moss-covered boulder that protrudes from the sea. I am sad and simply studying the depths. Suddenly, Berlyn bursts through the surface, plants a wet kiss on my cheek and vanishes. I recognize her immediately, even through the sheath of water that shrouds her. I felt her lips touch my cheek and the sensation of moisture on the side of my face.

Today's early morning experience was not so sublime. In my

dream, I am lying in bed with the awful feeling that there is an evil presence roaming my backyard. My intuition recognizes the evil as the same essence I felt on that black night when I arrived home to find Berlyn had been shot.

In my dream the telephone rings. It is Susan's friend, who confirms my fears by warning me in a slow wary voice of an evil intruder outside my bedroom window. I slowly crawl out of bed, spread the blinds apart with my fingers and am just about to look outside when Susan wakens me.

She says I have been howling in my sleep. Just then, I hear Morgan's little dog, yelping on the floor beside my bed. Apparently he's engulfed having his own nightmare. I waken him and he immediately leaps up on the bed and presses against me.

I am unsettled. I look out between the blinds into the backyard. Nothing is there that I can see. I retreat into my office.

May 1, 1992

It is my birthday, the first without Berlyn. I wonder how many more I will endure without her. I reread the message she wrote on the birthday card she gave me last year, holding the words in my heart. I suppose rereading her card will become a yearly tradition.

May 3, 1992

We have had several days of rain. The cool air is moist and sweet as I enter the park near my home late one evening. I feel a sense of relief being there. I crave isolation. Fog paints haloes around the orange glow of the street lamps, giving the landscape the look of a van Gogh painting. With Southern California gripped in a seven-year drought, the smells of damp earth and wet wood are notably refreshing.

I walk down the mountainside onto a baseball field and enter a boiling white cloud that has settled there. I feel at peace, wrapped as I am in the silent cocoon. I think for a long time about Berlyn and how she seems like a dream to me now—a dream from another life that keeps recurring. I think of how the tragedy of her murder has caused such disequilibrium in my life. I wince at the thought that the same disequilibrium has lead to perhaps the most growth I have ever experienced. I have a new relationship, it seems, and it is with disorder.

As I think further, it occurs to me that life's system is open to even the most minute dissonant influences that, in time, develop into what the system requires to sustain itself. I find that life's process does not protect itself from dissonance. Instead, it involves it, swallowing the change and digesting it into its strength.

The limited self I have made has always repressed disagreeable external forces for the sake of locking onto goals. Life, it seems to me now, is different; it is without a goal. It is self-organizing and embraces polarized influences without judgment or scrutiny. It simply is whatever there is. Everything that reveals itself is temporary anyway; only the process endures. It seems to me now that greater freedom creates greater stability and not the reverse, as I had been taught.

I am left with the feeling that balance and position are temporary states while continual process is eternal. All forms seem to be only temporary models on the way to becoming something else. Total equilibrium would mean death.

Random thoughts keep running through my mind. Memory of Berlyn surfaces again. It has become obvious to me that memory must supersede matter. Genetically speaking, information in memory, DNA, results in the production of matter. Because matter forms according to information, does it mean that energy is born of information, or is information born of energy? When information changes, dissonance occurs; old forms of matter disintegrate while new forms emerge and that requires energy. Was it the energy that caused the new information in the first place?

I think back to The Watcher's tale and remember the chain reaction of will—the first cause. It pervades everything, I think to myself. Will, I assume, is the catalyst. The identity that is produced, I conclude, must be nothing but information.

After an hour or so, a chilling breeze rushes down the mountain. My warm vaporous cocoon withdraws. I find myself standing near second base. The puddles, earth and grass appear for the first time. A star winks through a tear in the heavens and is quickly covered over again.

For reasons I cannot explain, I suddenly recall a scene from a nature program I had seen on television. A herd of zebra races from a watering hole as a lioness leaps from the underbrush and begins pursuit. A powerful swipe from the lioness on the buttocks of a galloping colt tumbles it to the ground in a cloud of brown dust. Running along side, the colt's mother veers away with terrified, glaring eyes. Her offspring struggles, flailing its spindly legs and blurting desperate cries to its mother, now on a rocky ledge out of harm's way. She calls back. The lioness tightens her jaws on the colt's throat and twists. It is over.

I think of compassion. Only humans have it. Life, or what I had once assumed to be God, is really indifferent to anything human. It was I who had assigned human meaning all these years. Life, I keep reconfirming, is simply a neutral process in which I am a temporary participant.

It occurs to me that this living process is a different form of intelligence than I. Being on the human frequency, so to speak, it is my guess that I will never really know life's true nature, but only my perception of it. I find that I cannot see past my own perception. I guess that is why life is relative to its observers. Seeing only my own perception, I wonder what really goes on.

I pause by third base. As a temporary condition of the process, I really have no control. No matter how I try to separate myself with reason, the process will have its way.

I wonder if anything really matters at all.

May 25, 1992

I pull another newspaper article from the bottom of the stack that is still on my desk. It has a photograph of Paul behind bars.

It brings to mind the day long ago when an inmate at the jail where I worked took a poke at a guard with a fork. It happened during lunch in the cafeteria. Guards immediately converged on the disturbance as if they had rushed from out of the walls. I was last on the scene. No one really bothered with me; I was considered an inexperienced kid.

The inmate who had attempted the assault was a broad-chested former boxer and a chronic troublemaker. He was awaiting trial for beating an elderly man nearly to death for thirty-seven cents. The old man's wounds required 130 stitches in his face alone. Two of the inmate's buddies entered into the melee that quickly ensued. The three black convicts fought against their captors to the cheers of the mostly black inmates that packed the room. In those days, the jail's inmates were continually teetering on the edge of a racial confrontation.

In seconds, three guards wrestled the inmate to the floor with the help of an illegal device one of the guards carried with him. It had a faucet handle like on a sink, with two curved metal fingers hanging down from a set of gears. When he clamped the contraption on the pug's wrist and turned it ever so slightly, he dropped to his knees like a sack of potatoes. Four guards behind plastic shields plowed the other two inmates up against the wall. The feeling in the room was tense. A fragile circle of guards held back a tightening circle of angry criminals.

They quickly put handcuffs on the trio and marched them from the room. I followed down a dimly lit gray hall to metal doors that were set into the brick wall near the infirmary. They motioned for me to open the doors. I did.

I had heard about solitary, but it was my first time inside. I found three cells. Each had a metal door that closed over a grate of bars, sealing out most sound and all light. The cells were only six feet deep by about four feet wide, with a metal bucket for a commode. They were located directly over the jail's boiler room so the temperature was stifling. Even the walls felt warm. Dead, stale air thickened my saliva, reminding me of the scent I had breathed at the zoo when I went there on a grade school field trip.

They lined the inmates up at the entrances to the cells and closed the metal door behind us. A dim sixty-watt bulb glowed from the ceiling. The boxer tensed as he stood between his buddies, his eyes darting from one of us to the other. I am sure he expected to be beaten—and he would go first.

"Okay, strip!" the short Napoleon-like lieutenant demanded. The inmates undressed and set their khaki uniforms in neat piles against the wall across from their cells. The lieutenant let them stand there naked for a few minutes, pondering their fate. "Open it up," he growled in a tone that suggested he was controlling his anger as well as the situation. The inmates quickly turned and opened the metal doors to their cells. "All right, inside." They stepped into the darkness. Guards slammed the doors behind them.

The lieutenant stepped outside and closed the metal doors, dividing the solitary cells from the regular population. He turned to me. "You are to check on them every two hours. You got that?"

"Okay."

"You turn on the light and check on them, then you turn it off, got it?"

"Yes, okay."

I checked on the inmates every two hours as I was directed. They had been sentenced to five days in solitary. On the second day, I noticed the tough guy was beginning to complain of back pain. Later that day he was crying, begging me to take him out. "They're crawl'n all over me. Millions of 'em. You gotta get me outa here, man, they're all over me."

The guys on either side of him asked nothing for themselves, only that I let out their buddy. I made a decision. It was Saturday; I would deal with the lieutenant Monday morning. I couldn't be sure, but I sensed the guy was losing his grip. Stench belched out at me as I opened the middle door. The inmate crawled out on his hands and knees, then with a moan slowly stood up. There were no bugs on him as he had claimed; he was just scared. He had broken. There was a glint of shame in his eyes. I let him keep his secret from the others. Just then, it dawned on me that I was closed in with a man facing serious prison time. I lowered my voice. "Okay, against the wall."

"Yes, sir. You'll get no problems from me. Nope," he mumbled under his breath, "no problems."

It was the first time in my young life I had ever been called "sir." I looked into his cell. Puddles of dark urine had collected on the uneven concrete floor. Feces were ground into his knees and elbows. He was no longer a tough guy. He wanted out and that was all. I opened the outside metal door to a rush of fresh air. I could hear the men in the other two cells sucking in the sweet new air from the point where the metal doors of their cells met the concrete ceiling. "Hose it," I demanded of the ring leader and opened the other two cells. Two naked men stumbled out, shielding their eyes from the sudden light.

They spent the next hour cleaning up their mess, then they showered. Later, I escorted them back to their cells in the jail population. I could sense a change in the boxer as I walked at his side.

His look became disdainful once again and he began to add a prideful swagger to his gait as tiers of caged men cheered him on. Only he knew the truth. He had the chance to realize who he really was and piece a real life together from there, but he ignored the opportunity. Instead, he slipped back into his fictional role. I closed his cell door and walked down the corridor as he yelled obscenities and threats at my back. He was returning a hero.

May 29, 1992

There are still two calendar days left in the current year in which I was with Berlyn the year before. Only two left. I do not know why such a configuration of dates seems to matter so much to me, but they do. There is something in the spring air, the angle of the sun's rays and the hot Santa Ana winds that heighten my memories.

My thoughts revisit an event that occurred just last weekend. It served to dramatically shift my view of the days surrounding Berlyn's murder. Each evening when I turned into my driveway, I'd immediately look to the front steps of my home where the hideous effigy had been placed a few weeks before Berlyn's death.

Since finding the effigy, I had felt uneasy, as if my family were under surveillance by a sinister person or even a coven of twisted people. At times, I would awaken in the middle of the night, on hearing a strange noise mingle with the wind, and would go directly to the front door where I expected to find another effigy, perhaps one meant for Susan, Morgan or me.

The object had been continually on my mind. Perhaps Berlyn's murder had been the result of a plot that employed some meta-physical power like witchcraft or sorcery that was represented by the effigy. Perhaps the man-made creature had been an omen of Berlyn's impending doom. Even though I had never believed in such things before, my desperation was an ideal breeding ground for superstition.

Last weekend, between basketball games at the park, I was lying in the shade of a maple tree, my head propped up against a basketball. The afternoon sun was intense, the grass cool against my legs. Just then, Morgan sauntered up with Kari at her side, one of the girls from the high school basketball team.

Berlyn had been in her junior year when Kari joined the varsity as a freshman. In fact, as she walked up the hill to where I was I could not help but recall the game in which she scored her first points. Berlyn had an easy fast-break basket that she gave up by making a slick pass behind her to Kari, who scored. Ever since then, Kari had been one of Berlyn's greatest admirers.

"Hey Dad, remember that old scarecrow that was hooked to our front door?" Morgan exclaimed. A chill raced through my body. Morgan giggled. "It was Kari, Dad. Kari and her friends hung it there as a joke on Berlyn."

Kari stood looking down at me red-faced and giggling. "Yeah, Berlyn once said the worst thing she could imagine was running over somebody with her car," Kari began to explain. "So, we were going to stuff the thing under her rear wheels, but when we got to your house, her car was gone so we ended up putting it on your door." She sat down next to me with a nervous laugh. "I hope you didn't mind."

Calm washed over me, sapping the strength from my arms and legs. I thought once again of the power of paradigms. "Kari, you can't imagine the relief you have given me in knowing it was you who put that thing there. Did you know that even the detectives investigating Berlyn's murder were looking for the effigy's creator to see if there was a connection to the case?"

Her grin faded away. "You're kidding! I had no idea."

I gave her an affectionate tug on the back of the neck. "Thank goodness it was you," I said as I lay back and closed my eyes, reveling in the relief.

Morgan and Kari ran off to play in the next game, but I sat out. I felt, suddenly, different about what had happened to Berlyn and my family. Finally, the specter of a metaphysical evil being summoned to kill Berlyn had started to fade. Her murder was now more societal than ethereal.

I thought about paradigms. As bizarre as it may seem, in those terrible days following Berlyn's murder, a parked car by my home late at night, a stranger in the shadows of a street lamp, moonlit shadows dancing with the hot wind, all aroused my suspicions. Were they linked to the great metaphysical evil that had killed my daughter?

From my experience, I have found that the greatest power a human has lies in interpreting life. All else, it seems to me, is subject to this one function.

I could feel myself melting into the grass with relief. Kari has given my reason what it needed to confront my paradigm. I felt a little like Dorothy in *The Wizard of Oz*, when, in the Emerald Palace, she threw open the curtain of the control booth to find a human at the helm, perpetuating the hoax of the great Wizard.

The turbulent furies I have been wrestling with released their hold. I could set my mind free to soar away from the awful assumption that had besieged it for so long.

May 30, 1992

It is almost the anniversary of the day Berlyn left our world. I am driving to the cemetery when I recall a time only a few weeks after Berlyn's murder.

Susan and Morgan were in New Mexico to immerse themselves in family. I was coming home from the office. Berlyn's crypt overlooked a manicured rolling green hill that I could see from the highway each evening.

I looked up at the hill as I approached, expecting the nightly ambush of remorse and depression to rush down at me from the summit. This night would be different. A mounting unsettledness began to overtake me. A panic attack of sorts, I thought to myself, but there was an undeniable force drawing me to where Berlyn was entombed.

Perhaps self-induced to reinforce the urging, a plea resurrected Berlyn's voice from somewhere inside my brain, "Come here, Daddy." It called out. "Daddy, come here right away."

I whipped across three lanes of commuters just in time to make a wild exit. The sun was beginning to set, signaling the cemetery would soon be closed. Ignoring pangs of self-doubt like I had that autumn day at the Chama River, I streaked through side streets following the challenge.

I sped past the towering black iron bars of the cemetery gate and drove up to the summit of the farthest hill. I parked and quickly climbed the steps to her tomb.

I whispered to her in a quivering voice, ignoring the doubt that raged within. Tears came to my eyes. I had set myself up for a devastating fall and the frustration of it all was overwhelming. I was talking to a slab of marble, not my daughter. Just then, I felt a strong hand on my shoulder. I turned with a start to find a short, stocky Hispanic man with a solemn face looking intently into my eyes.

"I'm sorry for you," he said in a heavy Spanish accent. "I read about your daughter and followed what happened on TV."

Then, with a slow nod, he motioned to a grave down the hill and across the road from where we were standing. "My boy, Carlos. He was murdered, too, just a few months ago. He was a wonderful athlete like your daughter. He played football. He was in his first year of college." His voice cracked, forcing him to a pause. He looked down and wept. Doing everything I could to hold back a flood of my own emotions, I could offer him little comfort.

He looked up, his jaw tightened, his gray mustache wrenching downward with his frown. "A bunch of guys were arguing in a bar over what part of Mexico was the best," he continued in a rough growl and shook his head in disgust. "One guy started shooting. Carlos was outside with his friends buying tacos from a vending truck when one of the bullets from the bar struck him in the neck. He died on the way to the hospital."

He went on to explain that he had been asked to leave the church during the funeral services for his son. He said he was drunk at the time and had raved openly against God for the injustice of Carlos' murder.

I put my arm around his shoulder and gave a gentle tug. Through our separate tragedies, we had entered a strange brotherhood. He was alone. His religion had failed him. I was alone too.

Suddenly, his expression softened, as if a great weight had been lifted from him. We embraced in silence and he left to sit by his son's grave. I watched him amble slowly down the hillside, then turned to Berlyn's crypt. I felt the purpose of what had drawn me here and I began to cry.

May 31, 1992

After lunch, I walk in the park near my home. It is warm, and the sky is unblemished. Sounds of Middle Eastern music come from gatherings of Iranian families on the far end of the grounds. Close to the ball field where I am headed, a table holds down a cluster of balloons straining to join the wind. A young mother and six or seven little girls are having a birthday party.

A scene catches my eye. It is taking place just outside the left field fence. The occurrence is not out of the ordinary. A boy of about thirteen in a soiled blue and white baseball uniform is walking hand in hand with a pretty girl about his age. She has long red hair, a pink sweatshirt and matching shorts. He looks almost out of character as all kids seem to in making the awkward leap from childhood to adolescence.

Seeing the young couple takes me back to that same left field corner one day when Berlyn was about fourteen years old. I had come to the park one afternoon to call her for lunch. I had stopped in my tracks about where I'm standing now. She was walking with a boy from her school, a fellow she liked. She was trying to muster the courage to ask him to the school's "backwards" dance, where the girl is supposed to ask the boy to accompany her. Just then, the boy reached down and took hold of Berlyn's hand. Pretending not to notice the change in their relationship that had just happened, they walked on with a slightly more exaggerated pace.

I could imagine the odd mixture of elation and embarrassment that must have erupted inside her. Then, she looked up at him and apparently asked the big question. He nodded. I smiled and walked back home. Lunch could wait.

About two weeks later, I found her upstairs in her room, lying face down on her bed. The lights were out and she was crying. Her long golden hair hung in the familiar ponytail that always waved behind her on the basketball floor. I walked in and sat on the edge of the bed.

"What's wrong, sweetheart?"

"Oh, Daddy, he got cold feet," she said haltingly. "He backed out of taking me to the dance. Now, I can't go. It's tomorrow after school, Dad, and I have no one to take me. I'll be the only one of my friends who's not going." She hid her face in her pillow and quietly cried.

I rubbed her back and spoke sympathetically, but I was of no real help. So I just rubbed her back for a while until she stopped crying, then kissed her on the cheek and left the room.

She would remain awkward with boys throughout her teen years, never being able to hide the telltale blushes that would rush onto her face and betray her.

Later, Nick began to call on her. I enjoyed talking with him about the films he was interested in making and he seemed to be kind to Berlyn. He was not the type that would overpower her; he shared with her instead, allowing her personality to surface and find meaning.

All this time, the real Berlyn was brewing. Somewhere in her adolescent experience, her feelings for boys became polarized. She used to call those whose lives were on a predictable course to success, "the boring ones." They were going to be bankers, dentists, businessmen, the kinds of mundane professions which, to her, were not daring or creative enough.

Instead, she developed an affinity for boys with whom she played basketball at the park. For the most part, they were good kids, but not the kind who had their lives already planned. These boys were still a mystery. They seemed, to her, to be more real than the others.

Then, she introduced us to Kenny, the young man who was to be her date for the prom. He was a junior at Berlyn's school, tall and stout, with brown hair that hung below his shoulders. According to Berlyn, he was not a good student and he did not play sports or excel in much of anything. Why did she like him, I wondered. The answer surfaced when Susan read a piece in Berlyn's diary after she was murdered. It simply said that she liked Kenny because "he's dangerous." I could almost hear her giggling when she wrote that part. I guess she never grasped how dangerous he would become.

Paul was one of Kenny's friends. Among the guns at the post-prom party was one that Kenny had lent to Berlyn's murderer. It was not the gun that killed her, but he had supplied a weapon to the stockpile that night. From my perceptions of him at the trial, I doubt that he was the dangerous free spirit Berlyn had supposed him to be. What I sensed was a young man who was very frightened of Paul and his entourage.

Following the murder, I heard from Berlyn's friends that Kenny was having a tough time at school. His peers had ostracized him for his indirect role in Berlyn's murder. I telephoned his mother to see if I could be of any help to him. His mother seemed eager for me to speak with him; she put him on the phone. We agreed to meet at Burger King.

I bought him a soda and we sat together in a booth by a window. It was the same seat I had sat in the day I gave Berlyn her car keys. I asked Kenny how things were going. He was very quiet. "Not too good," he admitted.

I changed the subject as a thought from the trial came to mind. "Could there have been any chance at all that the shooting was an accident?"

It was the first time since we had sat down at the table that he looked up from the straw he was crumpling between his fingers. "It was no accident." His words reverberated in my being like an explosion. He had been the kid who was asleep on the couch next to Berlyn that night. He was the one who woke up momentarily when Paul entered the room and noticed the gun pointing toward Berlyn before flopping his head back down on the sofa.

At that moment a group of six high school students, three girls and three boys, sauntered into the restaurant and sat around a large booth at the other end of the room. Their bubbly teenage demeanor suddenly vanished when they saw Kenny. They all stared at him with accusing eyes. I studied his reactions. It was clear that he had become used to ignoring the pressing stares of his peers. He did not even glance their way. He already knew he was despised.

I reached over and put my hand on his. He froze for a moment and stopped fidgeting with the contorted straw. "You made some pretty foolish decisions that night," I told him, "but you did not pull the trigger; Paul did. You did not kill my daughter; Paul did." He sighed and slumped forward a bit.

I never saw him again. I heard he eventually dropped out of high school and was finishing his degree in some remedial setting while working at a local retail store. I later learned that he and his family had moved out of town altogether. I hope I was able to help him.

On the way home, I recall my last words to him when he came to take Berlyn to the prom. "Take care of her," I said. He had nodded mechanically and then driven off. She never looked back.

June 1, 1992

I spend today alone with my thoughts.

June 2, 1992

Morgan asks me to take her for a ride up into the mountains behind our home. It is past her normal bed time, but I can easily tell it will be, for her, one of those nights that is going to be hard to bear. These will be the infamous first days of June. Sights and smells, the angle of the sun and the shadows it cast are all returning as reminders to the senses. Just the other day we watched the tuxedo-clad boy next door climb into a limousine with his girl friend and three other couples after pausing for a photo session on their way to their senior prom. Morgan's eyes appeared heavy and glistening.

We drive up onto a ridge and park. Far in the distance is the sparkling basin that cradles the sprawling city of Los Angeles. Then, there is the dark horizon where no lights exist at all—the vast Pacific ocean.

Morgan rolls down her window and leans against me. "Y'know, I think God is different to everyone." Her voice is soft as she looks at the distant lights. "I don't think God is what they taught me, Dad; know what I mean?"

I am amazed by my basketball player. She is a stunning, petite thirteen-year-old with a phone that never stops ringing and an army of boys and girls that fill our home on weekends. Suddenly, I am with a unique part of her that has rarely surfaced.

"You think God might be relative to each individual."

"Yeah, I kinda do. Since Berlyn died, everything seems different to me now. Even that tree over there is different, though it is the same tree I used to see. People, places, everything is different now, Dad."

Morgan's observation seemed every bit as much a matter of relativity as Einstein's—except her's is personal; meaning is relative to the observer.

Suppose a basketball player is traveling to a game on a subway train. He looks down at a spot on the floor and slowly bounces his basketball twice against that spot as the train barrels down the track. To a pair of observers stationed along the track outside, the player bounced the ball at point A and then again several hundred yards down the track at point B. However, to the basketball player inside the train, the ball bounced twice at the same spot. If not for personal relativity, individuality would seem a fool's game, an exception to the rule.

I think of something else. Big Bang theorists hold that everything in existence was once compressed into a timeless pinpoint of energy where all laws of physics stop. The energy is said to have exploded in every direction with a force so great that its effects have the bubble of our universe still hurtling through space. Perhaps our dimension is but one of the billions contained in the soapsuds like bubbles that shot outward with the initial blast.

Could it be that our finite universe is a bubble within a greater bubble? Could it be that there are bubbles within bubbles that occupy different dimensions of the same space? Could it be that the shell of the bubble of one universe is impenetrable to the life forms of another? Perhaps the shells of these dimensions can be traversed by the universal energy that may emerge from the unique transfiguration called death. Could Berlyn have passed through one of these walls?

Then I think, did the genetic information that was Berlyn create her life in its image or did life respond to that information by molding itself as Berlyn? Who was Berlyn? Was she an individual that participated in life or was she life participating as an individual? Is life not like a passing wave that became Berlyn only to vanish into the amorphous energy from which she emerged? Where, then, are all the personal relativities of her life that made her Berlyn? In the end, we perish and all that seems to remain is the collective tendencies of our species. But where is Berlyn? Was her life entirely encompassed by the physical matter of her existence? It is gone, but is she gone? Perhaps nothing really ends, but just transforms. Maybe somewhere there exists the energy that is the meaning of my daughter.

November 30, 1992

Today, I learn that Paul has been married in prison. The information comes to me from one of Berlyn's former classmates. I am infuriated. Events stemming from Berlyn's murder seem to have no end. I telephone California's victim-witness program. They, in turn, call the prison where Paul is incarcerated to inquire on my behalf. They call back to tell me that the rumor is true. He will also enjoy periodic conjugal visitation rights. I think to myself this guy took away all of Berlyn's rights, every one. He, alone, decided she could never marry or have the delight of her own children. He deprived her of an education, a career and all the meaningful experiences we mortals find in life. He decided that Morgan will never be an aunt, and that Susan and I will never be grandparents to children that resemble Berlyn. It seems to me that because Paul murdered her, Berlyn no longer has any rights at all. It is as if she had never been a member of the human race. Only Paul matters now. Only he has rights to be upheld and protected.

I am depressed further on receiving notice of Paul's appeal later that afternoon. I think about the position I will be in if he wins one and receives a new trial or lesser sentence. After all, I think to myself, he never awakened Berlyn that night to give her a chance to plead for her life. She had no appeal.

After the murder, society immediately swept in and took vengeance on Paul. That, I am told, is how modern society must function. I realized early on that an uncontestable pact between human society and me had been suddenly established. The pact was designed for society by society and being that I was a member, it was presumed that it carried my approval. Society would punish Paul according to its rules, relegating Susan, Morgan and me to simply being bystanders.

Another matter over which society took control was that of Berlyn's body. Because she had been murdered, an autopsy was mandatory. I remember sitting in the courtroom during Paul's trial listening to the County Medical Examiner testify to how normal Berlyn's liver and kidneys appeared when he removed them, and how much her brain weighed. I was stunned! I had learned from our funeral home that the state needed to examine Berlyn's body after the murder. But I had no idea they were going to hack her to pieces.

I remember condemning myself for being offended. After all, it was just her remains. Yet, to me, her body still represented something precious. It was Berlyn's personal form, the physical manifestation of a lifetime of memories. The small scar on her stomach, when, as a toddler, she fell on a lawn sprinkler, her powerful legs from years of competition in countless games, her teeth we had straightened slightly with braces, even the little wart on her shoulder, they all meant something to Susan, Morgan and me.

At that point, I remember wanting to grip Paul's throat with my hands and strangle the life from him. Because of him, strangers had torn open my daughter's carcass. Because of what he had done, they had even cracked open her skull and removed her brain. They had toiled over her like demons, butchering and measuring her in some macabre basement room. I could envision it taking place at the other end of a long dark corridor. Through it all, I had absolutely no control over them. I had no say. Paul had arranged for everything.

I acquiesced to the pact between society and me, first of all, because society is far more powerful than I am. Second because at the time I felt I was metaphysically responsible somehow. In those terribly confusing days, I had wanted to focus my attention beyond Paul on what I feared was the real hidden enemy, the father of all murderers.

Now that I have found there was no super-human evil presence leading Paul that night—except that which he had projected from himself—I find my attention returning to him as the stooge of his own illusions, the guilt being his and not shared with me.

Paul received nineteen years to life for what he did to Berlyn and will be eligible for parole after only twelve years, but he had sentenced Berlyn to death by shooting simply on a self-indulgent whim, without a trial or right of appeal. In essence, society's punishment of Paul was only 12 years while Paul's punishment of Berlyn was for eternity. I find such a disparity of circumstances to be the greatest inequity of all. However, it is an outcome I am bound by society's pact to accept.

Allowing Paul to marry and have conjugal rights seems a mockery of what society demanded of me. Now, I think to myself, he is appealing to be released from his sentence, claiming even his twelve-year sentence is unfair. It seems to me, he is concentrating more on escaping punishment than he is on the metamorphosis that might ultimately free him.

In effect, Paul has remained the same. Even murder has not moved him to change, and that is frightening.

What is most worrisome is the sheer boldness of Paul's demigod. Evidently, its raw savage power has been demonstrated to be beyond his control. To kill Berlyn, it exploded through his rational barrier that separated it from society. Now it knows the way out. It occurs to me that unless his rational barrier is considerably strengthened, or his demigod dies, Paul will kill again.

Should he wriggle out of his sentence, I would consider the pact between society and me to be broken. Then, I ask myself, what will I do?

Revenge is a fool's game. Paul could easily sweep me away from the life I have chosen on the whirlwind of the rage he has created in me. Only I can allow him such power. If I carry out revenge against him, society would surely hunt me down and lock me away from Morgan and Susan forever. Then, I think, my only human companions would be people in prison like Paul.

His murder of Berlyn has usurped so much of my waking and even sleeping moments that I rebel at the thought of giving him even a moment more. How, I ask myself, did he usurp the right to become the center of my life, the sun around which the fate of Berlyn, Morgan, Susan and I have revolved? It was by mindless violence.

My revenge, even if successful, would not change anything that mattered. It would not restore Berlyn to us or serve her in any way. It would be another act designed only for Paul, attributing to him additional value that, to me, he simply does not merit.

December 12, 1992

It is a crisp, cool winter day. Overhead, the sky boils with dark gray clouds. My blue T-shirt clings to my chest, saturated like a cold compress. My legs feel like numb appendages. A chill overtakes me as I stand next to the bronze plaque with Berlyn's name embedded in the basketball court. The team I am on has just won. Another team is warming up on the court to play us.

There are "pick-up" games where young men play three on a side or four against four on half the court. Once in a while middle-aged men can be found playing, but not very often. I am often the oldest player. Occasionally a girl can be found in a game, but only if she can effectively compete with men. Berlyn had been one of the rare ones who could not only compete against men, but humble some of them in the process. There are three outdoor courts in my town where a person can find a game, Berlyn's being the most popular.

I glance over at a tall, lanky sixteen-year-old leaning against a court-side tree. It is Mike, Paul's younger brother. I had felt his stare pressing against me throughout the last game. He now peers at me. It is the same look he had when our eyes met during the funeral. I try to read his emotions. He appears troubled. Fear, shame, anger, they were all there in his look, radiating through a tough adolescent veneer.

A fellow from the team I am on clasps my shoulder and says he has to leave. He had been a pallbearer for Berlyn. He casts a stern, discomforting glance toward Mike and leaves the court. We are now a player short and the opposing team is ready for action.

"Hey, Mike," I say with a nod toward the court, "want to play?"

His head jerks up, then he quickly regains his composure in the way a boy his age must. "Yeah," he says coolly as he slowly unfastens his warm-up jacket. "I'll run."

It is a three-on-three game. Later, I will not even remember who the third player is, but it does not matter anyway. In my mind, the real game is with Mike and me. We start play. I set a screen against his defender, then roll to the basket as I used to do with Berlyn. I reach up and there the pass is just where I need it. I make a reverse lay-up, putting us ahead.

Mike drives to the basket, leaps, I hit him with a pass and he scores. We are a team. Everything we do seems to work. We even cover each other's missed shots with rebounds. Hindsight has me feeling sympathy for the third player on our team because I wonder now if either of us ever threw him the ball.

We win our game and by now it is nearly dark. Mike nods to me, dons his jacket and ambles off alone. I walk into the park, talking to the clouds. Morgan will soon return to school. I hope she can weather it. We've done our best to help her heal. But who am I kidding? You don't heal; you simply change.

Susan is doing her best to find happiness in her new life without Berlyn. But when we go out on the town together, our conversations invariably find their way to our memories of Berlyn and we usually end up sad again by evening's end. I wish I could say all is well, but it's really not.

What do I do? Let life fulfill itself, I answer myself.

Everything I have done has perpetuated and enlarged a flaw

that is basic to the human condition. Together with my human family, I have wandered in a continually corrected course away from what works. Behind me is a patchwork of error and the shattered walls of an ancient paradigm. Ahead lies a new universe without identity—the stuff of hope.

I walk up a hill and I sit down between the gnarled roots of an old oak. I lie back against its thick, rough trunk and I begin to think about hope. I recall the hope to which I had awakened on summer mornings when I was young.

I ask myself, where is the excitable inspiration I had as a kid in the sacred forest? Will it be in the new universe? I believe now that hope and inspiration are available to whomever wishes to create them. They are all I have left of the laughing brook, the sacred forest and Berlyn.

One thing is for sure; I have found peace and a measure of relief since I set down religion's yoke and left the Garden of Eden. Life is the same in the wilderness; flowers still bloom and the birds sing. The fear and guilt I had experienced from the struggle of good and evil, I have since found to be my own projections onto life's neutral process. For me, the realization brings liberation.

It seems that everything that exists is part of a process around which my identity incidentally formed. Life is really what lives behind the mask I have made; I can tell because I have many inherited predispositions that it has mandated for me. As a result, it occurs to me that I am not a point in time, but an elongated process over many millions of centuries for which my current identity is at the leading edge. Even my own survival has been predisposed. I have to survive. It is already written that I will fight for my last breath as a human.

I also suspect that whatever I do during my brief appearance on the earth matters little. I simply express an interpretation of life's will. In a sense, the pressure is off; I am immersed in a process that is responsible for itself.

It has become evident to me that, with reason's concepts and judgments going before me, I separate myself from what I observe. My view, it seems, has been distorted all these years through the lens I made from reason. Even so, I feel an exhilarating rush of energy from the discoveries I have found and the remarkable freedom they evoke.

I do not know how close I have come to Berlyn, but I feel intuitively that she is in a dimension close at hand. All I know of where I am is that I am no longer where I used to be.

There is still the terrible sadness. Often when I am alone, just before sleep or when I am daydreaming, I see in my mind's eye Berlyn asleep in the darkness. I am hovering, it seems, by her side just above the mattress. A pale gray light suddenly washes over her. I watch as a silver bullet emerges ever so slowly from a silent flash of light in the shadows. I watch it rotate round and round, glistening in the dim metallic light as it searches for her temple. I listen to her last sweet breath. I remember her last day home, getting dressed for the prom. "How do you like my hair, Dad?" echoes in my mind as she walks proudly through the living room in her gown. I recall her last weekend with us turning the soil in our front yard and planting flowers with her mother. Then, I watch the bullet enter her temple. It must, you know. I close my eyes.

EPILOGUE

I remember a time when, as a little boy, I was walking across a snow-covered field. It was late afternoon. The sky was slate gray. A cold wind hummed through the pines of the sacred forest behind me. My dungarees were wet and cold as were my socks, but I was on a marvelous imaginary adventure. I would find warmth later with the setting of the sun, and home.

Suddenly, I came across a golden flower poking up through the ankle-deep snow. It was out of season and out of place, but there it was. I dropped to my knees, pulled off my crusted mittens and caressed it. My nose was numb, but I could still smell a little of its delicate fragrance.

I had a sense, even then, that the flower would soon die. It shouldn't be here, I remember thinking, not now, not here. It had come to life anyway and had opened itself to a cool winter sun. Perhaps it was here just for me, just for today, I thought. I remember feeling special to have shared a moment with the flower in the snow before it passed away.

SUPPORT GROUPS

There are a handful of national support groups that exist to provide help to parents and others who have suffered the loss of loved ones. Some of these groups hold meetings which may or may not be useful to you in your particular situation. I would also suggest checking your local newspaper, district attorney's office, and police department community services desk to see what other support is available.

Parents of Murdered Children
100 East 8th Street B-41
Cincinnati, Ohio 45202
Tel: 513−721−5683

Compassionate Friends
  National Headquarters
PO BOX 3696
Oakbrook, IL 60522
Tel: 708−990−0010

GRADS (Safe Proms)
PO BOX 868
Riverside, CA 92502-0868
Tel: 800−774−7237

Mothers Against Drunk Drivers
  (MAD)
5430 Van Nuys Blvd. #314
Van Nuys, CA 91401
Tel: 310−645−7260

Justice For Homicide Victims
PO BOX 2845
Malibu, CA 90265
Tel: 310−457−0030

California State Board
  of Control
Victims of Crime Program
PO BOX 3036
Sacramento, CA 95812-3036
Tel: 800−777−9229